This is Unimaginable & Unavoidable

"by Guy Smith"

NON-DUALITY PRESS

NON-DUALITY PRESS

6 Folkestone Road Salisbury SP2 8JP United Kingdom
www.non-dualitybooks.com

Copyright © Guy Smith 2005
Cover Artwork: John Gustard

First Printing May 2005

ISBN 0-9547792-5-8

Disclaimer; Thanks; Dedication

Nobody wrote this, and nobody is responsible for it. This 'nobody' is warmly thanked, and in particular the following guises it assumes:

Naomi Selby, Julian Noyce, Tony Parsons, J.J. Lothin and Tanya Davis, for all your terrific work with the manuscript; Stephen Cheeke, Phil Corkill, Sam Johnson, Naomi and Neera, for permitting the inclusion of our private emails in this public text; Tim Adams, Alex Armitage, Ed Bergin, Helen Brown, Robin Brown, Sam Cordell, Thea Edwards, Ceri Elliston, Lucy Elmes, Yara Fadayel, Tom Fisher, Richard Fletcher, Kirsty Gordon, Nat Goss, Philip Griessl, Helen Griffiths, Ross Hawkins, Thea Hincks, Madelaine Humphreys, Rachael King, Jon Kelly, Kamini Kishor, Danny Laird, Alex Lee, Roger Linden, Magnus Loutit, Catherine Maitland, Stephen Mercer, Sarah Rees, Tom Remington, Ellie Roylance, Seb, Gail Seres, Damian and Tean Smith, Jenny and Martin Smith, Fergus Waldron, Nadine Werner, Satya Zwecker, and the aforementioned, for love and encouragement.

This book is dedicated to Philip Corkill and Katie Sheard, for making this authorial nothing know that he is the most loved nonentity in existence: joint first with 'all the other' nobodies!

Contents

Foreword by Tony Parsons   9
Introduction   11

What Is Going On Here?   15
Here Are Some Little Black Squiggles   31
Reality Is A Timeless, Placeless 'This-ness'   41
What The Sense of 'Thought' Does   49
Choice, Rhyme, Sex and Nonduality   57
All There Is, Is Choice-less Awareness   71
There Is No Such Thing As 'A Woman'   83
Absolute Contentment Is Not A Possibility: It *Is* Reality   95
On Jesus, Christ, God And The Illusion of Objectivity   109
Love Loves   119
Enlightenment Has Nothing To Do With Suffering   127
There Is Only Supple Consciousness   133
There Is No 'Other'   143
Unity Has Nothing To Do With Unicity   157
Reality Is Holey-ness; All There Is, Is Dislocation   169
There Is No 'Mastery'; All Is Love   181
This Is Not 'An Excuse'   193
Some 'Deictic-Imaginative' Attempts At Revealing The True
Nature Of Reality   201
Heaven Is Here   209
This Is Unimaginable And Unavoidable   221
Sex And The Text   229
Oneness Is The *Only* Certain, Provable Fact   239
Selflessness Has Nothing To Do With Altruism   249
On Textual Hypnotism   265
Science Cancels Itself Out...& Reveals The Reality Of
Nonduality   277

Foreword

I love this book! It is passionate, uncompromising, irreverent, intimately openhanded and wonderfully without any sense of order or progression.

Throughout the whole work there is very little that the cunning guru mind can get hold of and turn into a belief system. There is a powerful invitation within these outpourings which seems to harbour and generate a feeling of the sensuous, the impersonal, the unbounded mystery that lies beyond the words.

This is not a book to wade through steadily, but rather a deep pool in which to dip one's foot . . . and maybe fall in.

There is a proliferation of so-called Advaita/Non-dual literature available today, and virtually all of it is borne out of a fundamental misconception about the nature of being. However, during the last decade some rare, clear voices have emerged out of the mist, and Guy's work is surely an inspiring and unique confirmation of this wonderful message.

Tony Parsons
www.theopensecret.com

Introduction

This text is best treated like a treasure-chest filled with diamonds, as opposed to, say, a treasure map. Conventionally a text operates through the sense of a sequential narrative in which something, some desired information, is progressively disclosed. Here, however, there is no sense of 'going anywhere' or of 'getting anything'. The text communicates directly, immediately – gesturing again and again to what is present, what is the fact, here, now, always and everywhere. Moreover, 'the text' is in actual fact nothing but a bunch of small texts that are by-and-large unrelated to one another. So, like examining the contents of a treasure-chest, there is no real 'order' here: please just dip into whichever passage takes your fancy, as and when.

This dislocated, disassociated textual form is designed precisely with the disabling of 'progression', 'movement' and the senses of 'being taught', and 'being in good hands', in mind. For, the sense that reality is divisible (spatially – as, for example, 'teacher' and 'taught', 'writer' and 'reader' – and temporally – as 'the beginning of the narrative' and 'the end of the narrative', 'prior to being in the know' and 'being in the know') is precisely the illusion this text seeks to expose and disperse.

Nevertheless, the sense that something, a thing of form and therefore of distinction and separation, is being 'grasped' in one of the texts, or 'pieced together', 'formed' amongst a number of the texts, may occasionally emerge. The diamonds, strangely cold to the touch, may seem to be slotting together to form some kind of mosaic. But, without fail, the mosaic will depict nothing, add up to nothing. You see, these 'diamonds' are in fact nothing but shards of ice, melting in your fingers and vanishing. This text, then, is not so much a treasure-chest as a bucket of water! Not such an appealing image!

So what is this bucket of water, this text, here for? In fact, this is the wrong question, and a symptom of the mind's neurotic tendency to suspect ulterior motive. This text is here; that is the fact. Just as life is here, life *is* – simply because it is! This book is just here, in these hands holding it.

So what will happen in the reading of this text? There are two possibilities. In both cases these little black squiggles will be translated into sounds, images and feelings called 'thoughts'. One possibility is that this thinking will not only appear but will linger as solid, continuous formations that are definite, definable somethings, and are therefore separate, abstract and limited. This kind of thought-formation, thought-stagnation, is known as 'ideation', 'ideology', 'belief' and 'doctrine'. Because it is formal and therefore limited and fallible, it is continuously threatened by doubt and death. Being formation, it is also separate and insular and therefore only itself: it cannot be the expression of anything else beyond itself. It cannot, say, express something called 'truth'. This goes for all ideology and doctrine: Christian, communist, materialist, whatever.

The other possibility is altogether different. As these little black squiggles are being translated into sounds, images and feelings, what may very well happen, periodically if not perennially, is that the sense of something beyond the thoughts, or rather *in* the thoughts and in everything else as well, will emerge. The thoughts will give way to this sense, this omnipresence. To dramatise this a little, it may feel like the pages being held and observed are bursting into flames and burning a hole in themselves, disintegrating in these fingers so that nothing is left. And the fire is not only in the black squiggles and the thoughts they conjure, and in the fabric of the book, the paper and cardboard, but it has caught onto the hands holding the book, the body sat here before it, and has filled and encompassed the entire landscape around it, leaving only one fire, oneness.

And what kind of little black squiggles is this collection of squiggles made up of? Signature words include 'oneness', 'unicity', 'nonduality', 'presence', 'consciousness', 'awareness', 'being', 'beingness', 'nothingness', 'emptiness', 'what is', 'is', 'isness', 'this' and 'thisness'. All of these words signify the same something, or rather no-thing, that this text is wholly and solely engaged in attempting to point out. The problem with language is that it pulls irrepressibly towards 'the something'. It shapes; it generates the sense of defined (perhaps multifaceted, yet) limited form, that which occupies a certain place and period in space and time. And what this text tries to express is that which is beyond form, is in all form, *is* all form, and is therefore formless, nothing.

It is the 'presence', 'consciousness', 'thisness' (pick any word from the list above!) in, to, and out of which all form appears.

Because of this communicative obstruction (the propensity of language to form) one will find that a disproportionately large quantity of this text (compared with other texts) consists of what is called 'deictic' language, language which points. This compares with descriptive and explanatory language, which functions through the solicitation of the sensual (for example, the descriptive 'green' operates by provoking the visual, the appearance of a colour) and therefore pulls towards the limited and the abstract, 'the thing'. Deictic language, on the other hand, can largely avoid this undesirable (in terms of communicating what this text seeks to communicate) 'imagination'. Rather than abstract, it gestures. The two purest and most helpful words for this are 'is' and 'this'. Nevertheless, it should be noted that even these terms convey, insidiously, the formal. 'Is', for example, defines, forms, specifies by generating the sense of a something, that is not a nothing, not an 'isn't'. With the word 'this', the problem is not so much the conveyance of solidity, as 'this' can be 'this nothingness' as much as 'this something' or 'these somethings' (though there is undoubtedly a tendency for the conditioned mind to assume that 'this' refers to 'a something'). The principal problem is that the very nature of gesturing conveys the schismatic of the formative: if there is pointing, something specific is being pointed to, and the senses of 'pointer' and 'pointing' are generated and excluded from this.

Having said all of this, imaginative, descriptive and also logical, explanatory modes of writing *do* have their own mechanisms for conveying the nondual; namely, as dramatized above with the fire image, through cancelling themselves out. This basically involves negating any sense of specificity that may be temporarily generated, rather like jotting something down and then rubbing it out, or proceeding to jot down so many other things that the page ends up saturated with black ink or graphite and nothing is said. Examples of this include, 'This "whatever it is" that is being expressed here can express itself as a sort of syrupy feeling, but since it is in all things, it *is* all things, it is all other feelings too'; and 'It is the seeing that there is only oneness…and it is also the "not seeing of this", and the thinking that there is only multiplicity and no indivisible oneness'.

That's enough words on words. This alerting you to the kind of textual mechanisms going on here is simply one way of promoting a general awareness of 'what is going on' that may (or may not) at some point manifest as the clear awareness of knowing exactly what and how reality is. This present awareness is the bursting into flames...

This text came about during the six-month period immediately after this absolute present awareness had made itself irrevocably known. Scattered throughout are four distinct literary forms. There is continuous prose, both typed and spoken (through a voice-activated word processor). There is poetry, which is often born out of desire for something more visceral than the primarily deictic prose, and as such, it comprises a good deal of sensual and sensuous content (particularly since the addictiveness of rhyme and rhythm appears to me synonymous with the pleasurable compulsion of lust and intercourse). A number of emails are included for the qualities of intimacy and ordinariness they convey, as these qualities can sometimes greatly assist communication. And, finally, there is a large collection of what have been labelled 'notices', which were primarily born out of two impulses: desire for relief from the congestion of prose, and the idea of creating promotional notices that would advertise nondualistic discussions I, at the time, envisaged holding in Bristol. As such, they are concise, telegraphic 'shots' or 'shocks' of expression, designed to provoke interaction and immediate, present examination. The writing of all these forms was exhilarating and like quicksilver. This contrasts starkly with all 'pre-enlightenment' experiences of authorship, which were unfailingly leaden, knotty and forced. I hope that this thrill and fluidity can be tasted and enjoyed in your reading of this, and that the fire, already there, soon makes itself known, crackles that bit louder, burns that bit warmer, glows that bit brighter...

What Is Going On Here?

1. What is going on here?

What is going on here?

Already, this is too fast,

Too suppositious.

Is something going on here?

Yes,

There is something,

This is something –

Isn't it?

So what is it?

What is going on here?

Is it true

That 'you are reading this text'?

What actually is the fact?

There is a sense of 'a text',

Is there not?

And the sense of 'a you'.

So both 'you' and 'text'

Are senses that are present.

And what does this perception imply?

It implies that this 'you' thing

Is not,

As it is often imagined,

That which experiences:

It is in fact

An experience,

Just as this book is!

Right now,

Is this felt,

Seen?

The sense of 'you'

May be something like

A murky shape, or a feeling of contraction,

Or anything else.

And what is implied

By the fact that this 'you'

Is an experience that is sensed,

And not 'the sensor'?

It implies that there is no such 'you',

Does it not?

If 'you'

Is just an experience,

Just as this book is,

Surely there can be no demarcation

Between a 'you' and a 'not you';

'An object' and 'a subject':

There is just sensation…

So that which has been labelled 'you'

Is nothing but a certain feeling,

Mistakenly labelled 'you'.

This is the fact.

This is what presents itself.

And since it is present,

It is registered somewhere,

Noticed by something –

Is that right?

For 'vision' to be, for example,

There must be an awareness of vision.

For anything to be,

There must be awareness, there must be consciousness,

That is clear.

If there is no consciousness,

Nothing is happening.

Therefore consciousness

Is omnipresent –

It is present in all things,

At all times,

For 'all things' to appear,

To be.

Consciousness is omnipresence…

It is not a singular, distinguishable, definable something:

It is in everything, it *is* everything,

It is this presence - here, now,

Always and everywhere.

So this is the real perceiver.

This is the real 'you'…

That formless, characterless, infinite no-thing…

(That which perceives that finite feeling

Mistakenly labelled 'me'…

And everything).

Knowing this as fact,

Knowing the substance of reality,

The presence that you are,

As infinite nothingness -

Beyond time and space,

Life and death -

This is the knowledge that you are untouchable,

Impregnable,

Immortal,

Flawless.

With this,

Comes fearlessness,

Fulfilment

And peace…

It is love,

Loving,

Without limit.

2. There is no such thing as 'spiritual practice'

There is no such thing as 'spiritual practice'.

That which is called 'meditation' is void. Recent wisdom has exposed all spiritual practice as an obsolete, self-defeating irrelevance.

There are basically two types of meditation. The more common and orthodox of the approaches comprises an unmoving body, silence and closed eyes. The less traditional approach, contemporarily favoured by scientists because of empirical research which suggests this method 'triggers meditative states' more readily and rapidly, for novices in particular, basically involves 'intense sensual stimulus' such as a brightly coloured image.

Both methods do the same thing. What takes place in both is a lengthening of singular sensual experiences. In the orthodox method the closing of eyes vastly simplifies visual sensation from, say, the appearance of a room, ceilings, walls, furniture, people, and so on, to something like 'a dark blur of swirling murky colours', and the same goes for 'touch', through the body's stillness. This not only comprises lengthier, more continuous sensate experiences in itself, but it also serves to slow down what is called 'thought' (which is actually nothing but a very fast moving procession of sensation) due to the reduced or less chaotic stimulus. 'Thought', then, is not actually a different faculty or reality to 'sense'. It is just a word given to a particularly rapid flow of clusters of sensation. For example, the thought 'penguin' consists of visual senses of black and white, a sort of egg-shape, and waddling; aural senses of crunching snow and some sort of squawk; and the feeling of softness and wetness perhaps.

In the second approach, the 'intense sensual stimulus' involves a particularly arresting experience (orgasm springs to mind as the most obvious example of this - something that has been utilised by Tantra), which captivates attention directly and wholly - again, replacing rapid, chaotic sensate shifting with a singular, lasting sense.

What both meditation approaches ultimately boil down to, then, is the production of a slower, smoother sensing; a slower, smoother reality (the same is true with 'prayer', incidentally: the chaos of normal thought is supplanted by a slower, smoother single, stately discourse). What can then come about is what has been termed variously 'peak experience', 'the transcendental', 'the mystical' and 'meditation' (incidentally, it is essentially the same experience as 'psychedelia', 'the trip'). What this consists of is purely the seeing that there is only sensation, that reality is nothing but sensation. To the perception conditioned by belief in 'an external world', a reality split into 'sensor' and 'sensed', this unicity seems extremely radical...it is a perception in which everything may seem to melt and bulge and warp as one syrupy substance called something like 'awareness' or 'consciousness'. It can be a very blissful perception, not only because the 'psychedelic melting' is a great relief, a collapsing of hard, tense, objects, but also because it involves the intuitive knowing that 'I am this omnipresence, which, being in all sense, *being* all sense, is infinite and immaculate'. This is a serene, fulfilled and fearless understanding.

The meditative perception is almost perfect...but not quite. And this 'not quite' is an infinite, seismic, existential difference. With meditation there is inevitably the sense of a process. Meditation *is* a process; without 'process' there can be no such thing as meditation. For meditation to be anything, there has to be the thought, 'now I am going to meditate', followed by the sense 'now I am meditating: there is something called meditation which is a specific, singular something, and I am currently doing it, experiencing it, being it'.

Meditation is the sense that the lush seeing that 'all is sensation' is at the end of some particular practice. But that particular practice, the process, is nothing but sensation: there is only sensation. So why bother with the process? 'The process', 'meditation', is but an illusion that sensation is somewhere else, that there are 'separate things' called, for example, 'processes', 'no process' and 'end of process'...

But all there is is sensation! There is no process, no meditation, no 'spiritual practice'.

One final concept to behead! One might say, OK, that's fine, but if certain events such as closed eyes, still body, silence and vivid sensate stimulus happen to produce a slower, smoother flow of sensation that is pleasurable – surely this has value, has its place?

It does not. Once it is seen that there is only sensation (which can happen at any moment, and which the belief in meditation can only obscure), sensation is incomparably slower, smoother, juicier. If it is seen that there is only sensation, which is omnipresent, and I am that, all the effort invested in keeping the illusion of a solid, structural universe, with a solid structural 'me' at its centre, is obsolete – supplanted by the far more warming, satisfying, freeing knowledge that I am infinite, indestructible and integrated in existence beyond integration: there is just indivisible oneness. And, with all the anxiety, guilt, blame, rationalisation and affirmation of 'the me' wiped away, thought tends to be just the smooth, succulent fluidity meditation seeks. But meditation can never reach such a state. Its very formulation ensures this completion of sensate freedom is denied. Meditation involves the belief that there is something called 'meditation', and that separative sense is the nature of incomplete seeing, and dissatisfaction.

It is so simple. There is just 'this'. There is nothing outside sensation: examine this; see that this is so.

And that is it. 'The me', 'the world', 'the other', 'the object' all collapse, dissolve…into the timeless, placeless primeval soup of sumptuous sensing, pulsing presence: 'this'.

3. How dualistic expression masquerades as nondualism

It beggars belief just how badly the nondualistic perception is communicated. Last night I was looking on 'nonduality.com', which has a good deal of intelligent material by the way, and one of the things on offer was an audio-clip of a teacher supposedly talking on nonduality (I can only assume... considering the website) and he was talking absolute nonsense! He said so many nonsensical things that I can only remember a tiny fraction of them. He said something like 'Humans are the only creatures we know about who are capable of consciously tapping into oneness', and he also said that 'Oneness', which he often described as 'stillness' and 'peacefulness', 'is there between the words [his words and all words presumably], there between the thoughts, there where thoughts are not obstructing'. I'm struggling to remember just exactly what was said, simply because it was so inaccurate. It just doesn't make sense.

Thought is not some kind of obstruction to oneness; neither are words. What kind of 'oneness' is 'here and not there'; 'here' 'in silence' and 'not there' 'in thoughts and words'? Thoughts are oneness thinking; words are oneness appearing as words. Nothing can obstruct or disturb what is always and only the case.

This needs to be looked into more intelligently and more precisely because the actual stone-cold fact of the matter is that there is no such thing as 'a thought' or 'a word'. Let us take for example the thought or word 'sun'. Look at what actually is the case. This needs to be done very precisely, very simply. So we have the thought-word 'sun': what is there? Well, there's the sound 'sun', 'sun' is a sound, it's something heard. If you're literate, there are also three little squiggles of ink on a piece of paper. Then there's the visual image of something like, say, a golden, yellow, white sphere or circle. And then there may be the feeling of warmth, or maybe burning. So we have visual black squiggles, a visual yellow circle, a feeling of warmth or of burning, and the sound 'sun'. Now where is there any connectedness in that? Where is there any 'thought' or 'word'? Where is there any 'sun'? The way most brains are conditioned, these things are assumed to be not only 'connected', but 'one thing': but this is just another separate, dislocating arising called 'a sense of unity'. And that's just a sense, a feeling. So here's our list: we've got the black squiggles, we've got the yellow circle, we've got the feeling of warmth, we've got the sound 'sun', and we've got a feeling of 'unity', but all of these things are there, they are just present, and there is no relation or connection between them at all: that's just imposed by the feeling of unity which is only yet another appearance that's totally suspended and dislocated from the others.

The reason I've highlighted this in so much detail is because it's a useful demonstration for seeing how when something's looked into, when it's seen that there's only sensation, the whole of reality falls apart. This doesn't exclusively have to be done with 'a thought'. Take, for example, this book here, in your hands. That's not a thought, that's not something that's been evoked by the mind. In a way it's no different...but here it is, anyway. You say 'book' but actually, what is the case? There's a seeing of rectangles and also squiggles, there's white and black, there's a feeling of weight, a feeling of papery-ness, and then there's the movement of thought (these particular disconnected clusters of sensations), which tends to happen when the black squiggles are being scanned. Again, there's nothing left; there's no 'book'. It all just collapses. And this is the seeing of oneness. The funny thing about this is that, to the mind (not that there is 'a mind', 'the mind' is just another nothing – but speaking always depends upon projecting some false definition or another), this can sound dualistic. The mind may think 'This isn't pointing towards oneness, this is pointing towards the most extreme separation and dislocation imaginable'. This kind of mental response reflects one of the fundamental misconstructions. The misconstruction is that unicity, which is nonduality and oneness, has something to do with unity, which is harmony, integration, grouping. But unicity is not about lots of parts fitting seamlessly together to make a unified whole. Unicity is indivisible. It is not about something holding together; it just is oneness. And this is one of the points where a discourse must simply go quiet, because nothing more can be said about it. It's frustrating because it hasn't been fully explained: but such fullness is impossible because explanation and description in verbalisation function through definition, and unicity is the undefined and indefinable appearing to be definition...though actually, as was illustrated above, as soon as any seemingly defined thing is examined, it is seen that there is actually nothing there whatsoever; no solidity, no body.

The other thing I mentioned from that audio-extract was a statement along the lines of 'us being lucky enough to be humans, since humans are the only creatures we know of that are capable of consciously tapping into oneness'. Now this is inaccurate for all kinds of reasons. It is just woefully, recklessly misconceived. Oneness cannot be 'approached' or 'tapped into'. Oneness is the case. A cat is oneness cat-ing. A rock is oneness rock-ing. Humanity appears in oneness; humans cannot tap into oneness; humans *are* oneness appearing as humans. Oneness is the seeing that there is no such thing as 'a human', 'a cat' or 'a rock': there is just sensation. When consciousness knows and sees that there is only itself, there is the seeing and knowing 'I am not this body, I am not these thoughts; neither am I that cat walking around over there or this grass growing over here'. All of this simply happens, but it happens to nobody and has absolutely nothing to do with 'being a human' or being anything else. It is non-selective, and it is beyond 'shape', 'form', 'definition'.

So can you see how stupendously inaccurate some of these supposedly nondualistic expressions are? They compress and compound, very often, the sense of 'things' like nothing else, in that they *seem* to be doing the opposite, but aren't. So it is an insidious affair. Just in the little bits I've remembered and described, suddenly you've got 'humans' as solid, formed entities, you've got 'oneness' as a something located somewhere that can be tapped into, the 'tapping into it' as a process that's a formal something, you've got this being undertaken 'consciously', which becomes some specific, distinguishable 'state of mind' to do with 'choice' (yet another solid something) and all that rubbish. And then by implication you've got 'non-humans' – so, 'animals' and 'plants' and 'rocks' – as solid, separate things. And in the first example you've got 'thought' as something formal and separate to 'silence', which then becomes something solid, defined, too...and it just goes on! And this is the illusion creating itself, over and over again, and that's fine and playful and it's the whole game, and it's what the appearance of creation is all about. But it's the essence of dualistic perception and expression – which is misconception.

4. How nondualistic expression corrupts as dualism

The difference between nondualistic expression - true, pure nondualism - and duality is very simple and easy to spot. All organised religion is dualistic. There happens a something called something like 'Jesus', Jesus who is a temporary, mortal form - a body, some thoughts and feelings that come ago - that exists in a specific place in space and period in time (apparently). That happens, and then words from lips start pointing towards that which is omnipresent, beyond form, eternal. And what these words say is that the real nature of reality has to do with something called "God", which is omnipresent, infinite, beyond space and time. Then the temporary body gets nailed to a cross and dies, and everyone else gets hold of these words and thinks 'Oh right, there's something called God that's infinite and omnipresent – and obviously we're not that, because we're not omnipresent or infinite; look, I'm just this funny little body here'. So a division takes place: there's God on the one hand, and then there's everything else on the other hand. And that's duality – suddenly you've got a distinction being made between something called 'matter' and something called 'spirit'. And then all kinds of weird and wonderful practices spring up: abstaining from 'earthly things', 'things of the flesh', trying to distance yourself from 'the temporary' in order to obtain 'the timeless'. And the word 'omnipresence' has been totally overlooked. Omnipresence is the key here. God is omnipresent. If God is omnipresent, then God is flesh, God is sex, God is a materialist, God is materialism, as well as everything else. God is absolutely unavoidable. And God is not God. In other words, God is not a defined something that is separate. So when the word 'bed' is said, or 'television', this is what God is, or 'wall' or 'ceiling' or 'mobile phone' or 'dildo'. This is all God; there is only God.

And the word 'God' has become so conceptual, such 'a thing', it has become unusable. So words like 'awareness' and 'consciousness' are preferable. And not only for this reason, but also because words like 'awareness' and 'consciousness', as the new God, sound more intelligent and less believing than Jesus' vocabulary (to contemporary ears). And with the words 'awareness' and 'consciousness', although they too have their own pitfalls, reality, which is seen and known in awakening, can be witnessed at the drop of a hat, without anything needing to happen. Of course this must be so, since reality cannot be approached, this is always and only reality, but the words 'awareness' and 'consciousness' appeal to the modern mind, and also keep things nice and simple. Minds, conditioned as they contemporarily are, already know, by-and-large, that everything that is experienced is experienced in and as consciousness. Scientists know this; philosophers know this. But they know it as a learned fact that is stored in the memory, so it is not felt experientially, or - to use a more accurate word, since 'experience' implies 'a subject', 'a person', 'a form', who experiences - existentially.

What nondualistic communication is all about, then, is allowing this ('there is only awareness') to be known directly in terms of perception, continuously or rather timelessly, rather than in terms of stored knowledge occupying a particular limited space and time. Nothing needs to happen for this, and nothing can happen for this, because there is just perception, and this is only ever the case. So it's funny: on the on hand one talks in terms of 'awakening' and 'seeing the true nature of things', which sounds unavoidably like an event, a happening; and on the other hand, when it happens, or rather, when it doesn't happen, it is known that nothing has ever happened, nothing will ever happen, and there is only ever 'perception', or 'oneness'.

5. Before Jesus was, I am

Before Jesus was, I am;
For 'Jesus' was 'a mortal man',
In time born, of space formed,
And vanished in the limits of a lifespan.

'Before Christ', is the myth of the Christian,
For 'Christ' is not a form or a system;
The Absolute bears no relations,
Was never born - *is this*; this radiance…

Before Guy was, I am
(The same holds true for that labelled 'you'),
For I am not 'a conscious man';
Consciousness is what I am.

Here Are Some Little Black Squiggles

6.

'Narration' suggests 'narrator',

So 'narrative' is better:

Narrative, like 'Guy Smith',

Is but a load of letters.

7. This is just text here

A special gift is manifest here. The gift is this: the total inability to write to a plan. A few days back, here was a completed outline for what was to be the most incisive, daring, dynamic book on nonduality imaginable. Sitting down to actualise the plan... zilch.

So, all that can be done here is to write. Though we have met already (indeed I have introduced myself on several occasions - for example, as 'not a conscious man', 'consciousness', and 'just a load of letters') I would like to introduce myself again. The problem is, there is no one here to introduce. Can you see this? There is just text here, just ink. It can be very convincing that there is a somebody somehow 'in' these words, addressing you now, telling you something... but look clearly, and you will see that there is nothing but ink on paper, and the movement of thought.

8. Identity is image; image is nothing

I, mage; I'm age;
Image of a wise old sage,
Imbedded deep within this page:
This is what I say.

I, mage, as time and space,
Am but the banshee, of this white sheet;
This flat stage, abandoned, unmade:
Free from 'you and me', I'm afraid.

9. I am but ink

Getting to know someone
Is such a bore,
Such a chore;

It's why I put down a book before
Narrator and character
Are barely born.

Do you agree?
Or in reading this,
Do you feel you know me?
Precisely because
You see as I see?

You don't know me.
You suppose I am
'A somebody',
Placed behind a nose.
Look closer,
Do not think,
And you will see,
I am but ink,
Pretending to host
A boring ghost,
That is in fact unborn.

10. Little black squiggle formations

One thing about poetry is that it appears to embody a particular expression in a manageable, observable, digestible form. Compared to prose, a poem can give the impression of being an artefact, like Keats's 'Grecian Urn', or a personality: an object or a subject. In fact, this is a mirage. There is nothing there: no centre, no body, no somebody, no unity. No 'poem', in fact. Suddenly there is nothing to manage, observe or digest – 'I am but ink'.

Yet the sense of a somebody - a narrator, or a writer - is ferociously convincing and persistent to the mind conditioned by the dogma of separation. By 'the dogma of separation' I mean the belief that there are 'somethings' called 'individuals' who wander around separately in what is called 'a material universe'. There is 'a you' sitting here holding this book. 'This book', then, is part of that 'material universe' that is separate from you, and 'out there'. So that, even if it is grasped that there is no one here, that I am just text, this is solely text, the belief lingers, 'But someone out there *did* write this, this *is* or *was* the expression of a somebody, at some point in time'.

The truth is, nobody wrote this, just as there is nobody here, now, saying this. And it is exactly the same with what has been labelled 'you'. You are not reading these words. These words, the sense of eyes scanning them, the notion of a brain registering them, the place in which this appears to be going on, is all going on in a perception which is what you are. Confusingly, included in the pure perception can be the sense of 'a perceiver' and in this case 'a reader'. But this somebody or something is nothing but an artificially segregated bunch of unrelated occurrences – say, thinking, sensation, the sense of a particular body – that, like absolutely everything else (this book, the ground below) is made of perception, is purely perception.

Notice that one of the qualities listed (imagined to be one aspect of this 'me' thing) – 'sensation' – is in fact not something that could possibly be placed or identified at all. That which is believed to be 'the outside world' that is 'sensed', experienced by sensation, is in fact nothing but sensation. This book is the vision of rectangularity, the feeling of papery-ness and weightiness…it is purely sensation. Likewise, that which is imagined to be 'the sensor', the someone who is experiencing sensation, and by extension some imagined 'outside world' through it, is also actually nothing but sensation…a certain feeling, the sense of some structure. There is only sensation. There is nothing else. *You* are sensation; *this* is sensation.

The segregation, and in fact fantastical creation, of 'sensor' and 'sensed', 'me' and 'not me', is nevertheless highly compelling, and relentlessly and insidiously so. Consider the phrase 'I am nothing but this text'. To a degree, this is a vigorous, energetic expression of the nondual: it says 'There is nobody in here, no identity, no somebody, here is just text'. Much of the vigour, the impact, of the phrase stems from the drama of beginning with a seeming assertion of selfhood - 'I am' - before immediately vaporizing this sense by pointing out that there is 'nothing but this text', no somebody saying or writing it. It is creation and annihilation in one literary stroke, which actively demonstrates, performs (always a more gripping mechanism than the abstraction of description and explanation) both the incredibly convincing believability of the self, and also the non-existence of that imaginary someone. Yet, despite this dramatic revelation, a subtle duality is nonetheless communicated. While the 'I am' tops itself, 'this text' propagates selfhood all over again. 'A text' is the idea that several hundred thousand black squiggle formations, also known as 'letter and punctuation marks', are somehow also one overriding 'thing' called 'a text'. This 'text' like the 'I am' is imagined as some permanent or at least continuous something that is 'there throughout the black squiggles'. Take away the paper, the letters and punctuation, or keep them in place if you prefer, but you will never find any 'text' there. The expression 'this text' evokes the conditioning of separation by making a disconnected, purely present, bunch of figures (the aforementioned squiggles) appear as a distinct, crystallized, singular object, somehow cordoned off from all other sensory arisings. This is the illusion, the mirage.

11. Oneness is oneness···

So this is oneness speaking, oneness writing. And oneness is the writing and oneness is what the writing is saying. Words can mislead, in this context of trying to express nonduality, only if exclusively 'what the words are saying' is listened to, and what the words *are*, is overlooked. Ink, sound, breath, sensation. Oneness can never be compartmentalised. Oneness isn't oneness; oneness isn't nonduality; nonduality isn't nonduality. As soon as a word is used to describe this, a sense of definition is conveyed, a sense of specificity, a sense that 'this is it; it is this – and so it is not that'. To make it an 'it', a something, an object, is erroneous. And yet with words this is unavoidable.

Sitting here in bed, on a cold winter's day, in an attic room with no insulation above it, wrapped up in two quilts, having just woken up, with a pleasurably warm, fuzzy feeling - oneness appears to be these quilts. I am always wrapped up in oneness. Oneness is my refuge, my warmth; my body and my body-heat. Oneness is my lover, and my Guardian Angel. And oneness is everything. Oneness is there in divorce; oneness *is* divorce. Oneness is a bad cold and terminal cancer. Oneness is slicing an onion and slicing one's finger off. And so it is the most wonderful thing, because no matter how dire or painful or trying the circumstances, it is the case, it is present, it is the presence of the case, the circumstance. And so it is the mightiest, utterly unmovable shoulder to lean on. Of course, *I am* that shoulder, there is only that shoulder, but it is enjoyable to dramatise and poeticise this as words, as doing so can convey a particular response to the feeling and seeing of this oneness. In this case, it is the sense of being protected, embraced, accepted...without the slightest threat of being abandoned, betrayed, cut-off.

12. Dualistic perception is oneness (perceiving dually)

Some have raised the issue of what would happen to the enlightened perception if, for example, serious brain-damage came about, through, say, a car accident. The most honest answer I can give to this is 'I don't know'. I don't know if conditioning could be re-imposed and cause a clouding-over of this awareness of awareness, if some extreme conditions were imposed upon it - somewhat like the infant being educated in 'materiality', 'selfhood' and 'separation'. The difference between the awakened perception and the perception of infancy is that the former both *knows and is* knowingness, while the latter *only is* knowingness. So the latter is far more easily corruptible. But if, say, a car accident reduced the brain to an infantile state, perhaps it could be reconditioned to the separative perspective once more? I don't know. What I do know is that whatever happens is oneness. I know that I have never been a single step from oneness, nor can I ever be. So even if this knowingness, which is so clear, so obvious, so natural, were somehow to cloud over, due to extreme circumstances, I know, here and now, that that cloudiness, that confusion, will be pure oneness, radiantly immaculate; and that, at some point, the thoughts, the body, the emotions, the sensations, will drop away once more and confusion will dissolve into brilliant purity, luminous presence. This is called 'death'.

I am presence. This is presence – and there is nothing else. You are presence. Presence is presence. This book here, in these hands, isn't made of paper or chemicals or atoms: it is made of consciousness. It is made of the presence that you are...as are these hands that are holding it, as is this sense of room, space, environment. This is presence. This is consciousness. And consciousness is not located anywhere, it is the omnipresence that perceives everything, that sees what it sees. Consciousness is non-selective, non-discriminative. It sees sky, it sees buildings, walls, it sees the television and what's on the television, *The News*, *The Simpsons*, it sees this body here, and other bodies, it sees thoughts, it sees anger and frustration, and joy, valuing and criticism. And it does not segregate these into any 'me' and 'not me', any 'object' and 'subject'; all of these happen in consciousness without any hierarchy, any valuing taking place. It is not consciousness that separates, or appears to separate. Separation is a temporary perspective that is here one moment, gone the next; here one life, gone in death. So, whether you see this as 'a book', a separate, objective, external thing, or as an appearance in consciousness (which is the truth), the awareness of all of this is 'there', present, eternally ready. You don't even have to go looking for it. In fact, looking for it is the nearest you can get to avoiding it, though really it is unavoidable. That which is called 'avoidance' is it, so there is no such thing as avoidance. You are that: it is already the case. Nothing needs to happen. This is it. The belief you carry that something needs to happen, that you need to get somewhere, get something, or lose something, is misinformed, is confusion. And yet it is that, it is oneness. Just relax – the task is already complete.

Reality Is A Timeless, Placeless 'This-ness'

13. An account of experience one week after awakening

Clarity glows like a radiant mist that in fact demystifies and brightens, sometimes almost unbearably so. It is a luminous presence; it is a sheen and a shimmering. It is a collapsing into light. One walks the streets energised…seeing all the appearances of life thinner and more fragile than painted eggshell or coloured foil. Yesterday, as I returned from work looking geeky in shirt and shoes, glasses and wafty hair, I glimpsed a group of young men heckling me and sticking their middle figures up at me from an upstairs flat. And where was the fear? Nowhere to be seen! It was just immaculateness demanding my attention: 'Here I am – I love you,' it shouted! This sense was so intensely felt that even a mischievous subsequent wish that I could have stared more lengthily and lovingly into those flashing eyes and erect fingers happened and repeated several times.

Still I awake to that frazzled, jaded, separate feeling, and find the mind occupied with combating the implicit doubt that 'it hasn't happened' with affirmations that desire a future emergence of oneness. And then it is realised or rather remembered (for the umpteen billonth time!) that this frazzled, jaded, separate feeling *is* it, *is* enlightenment, *is* oneness – and then funnily enough (and so I guess strengthening the false belief a little) the lush, fresh, lightness tends to seep immediately from everywhere!

Sometimes this lush, fresh feeling, the taste of oneness, actually feels undesirable… well almost! This is a refreshing revelation – as it counteracts a little the compulsive, needy leaning towards this blissful experience; a leaning that marked 'pre-enlightenment', and lingers as a sort of mechanical, habitual residue still. This is it, whether it be luscious relaxation and light, or fear, uptightness, defensiveness and egotism, or the striving for a particular experience… it is all and only oneness.

14. Identity is an absurdity

If glasses are
'An intelligent man',
If glasses are 'a nerd' -

Identity,
You must agree,
Is totally
Absurd.

15. There is no 'psychological depth'

Sex.

The idea has happened that a losing of interest may be manifesting itself and there is almost nothing that slays such an undesirable onset as effectively as these three particular black squiggles (s e x). Fear not. Whenever this attention-slipping is imagined some form of this 'sex' stimulant shall be administered, without fail!

The propaganda is that there is a something known as 'the other', which generally invokes fear. First, for example, it is imagined that 'I am male' and suddenly a mysterious, unpredictable, irrational and hysterical nightmare called 'female' is born. But this is not exclusively a 'sexual identity' thing. Consider, for instance, the impact on the belief in being a very humble, ordinary creature, the notion of 'A Hollywood Star', 'Einstein', or 'The Guru' has. The fear is that there is someone so unbelievably special - strong, courageous, charismatic, intelligent, sensitive, enlightened, mysterious – 'in there', that the someone 'in here', 'me', is woefully inadequate in comparison. But there is no one in there. There is no one in here, as these squiggles keep pointing out. There has never been such a thing as 'a guru' or 'a master', let alone a particularly holy, insightful or radical one. The Hollywood star is not the terrifyingly beautiful, graceful, mesmeric being she appears to be; she is purely *this*, what you are, appearing. She is not even a she. There is just this – appearing as beauty, form, fear. Where is there any 'her' or 'me' in this? There simply isn't. There is only sensation. When this is seen the fearful response tends to disperse, by itself, slowly or quickly. Since it is seen that there is no one, that all these imagined pockets or capsules called 'somebodies' supposed to be walking around, living lives, are in fact mere phantoms, nothing, just sensations misconceived, the pockets of fear for these nobodies correspondingly collapse. But it doesn't really matter if they don't. Fear is now seen as an uncomfortable, yes, but really harmless sensation that comes and goes…

The poem above states, 'Getting to know someone / Is such a bore / Such a chore' (See p.35). Two things spring to mind in response to these lines. First of all, this 'getting to know someone' is only 'a chore', or anything at all, when it is thought that there is someone to get to know. Yes, effort may happen, but with the realisation that there is no great psychological depth, no unfathomable enigma, sitting across the table from you, a sense of being seeing everything, knowing everything (just light, supple configurations of sensation happening), a consequent ease and content may occur.

The other thing that springs to mind is that this 'non-process of not getting to know no one' – becomes far less of 'a bore' or 'a chore' when that nobody happens to be a leggy blonde or a bronzed Latino! A light, clearly depthless limerick on this subject:

16. Dramatising impacts of belief in identity

Ah! The English Rose.
The enigma no man knows.
The Lady, The Beaut,
Who by repute,
Is frigid and easy both.

Now which of these fair?
And which is true? Who cares!
When online,
A Latino 'of mine',
Leers in underwear…

17. Dismantling the spectral textual time-machine

The apparent narrator of the poem bypasses the daunting effort and fear of trying to face and permeate 'enigma', the imagined 'real woman', in favour of the guaranteed access or success of internet pornography. If only he realised that there is no 'real woman', no intimidating, unknown enigma 'in there', then the realm of real sex might be just as easy, accessible and welcoming as cyber-sex. Perhaps not!

This free-fall writing, this ad lib thinking, the result of this aforementioned 'gift', is most suited to the expression of the nondual. Firstly, when the subject, the 'me', vanishes, or at least topples from his throne, his centrality (so that instead of things appearing to happen to me, 'me' happens, if at all, to awareness, in awareness - as just one of the many appearances happening), thought somehow feels more 'light' and 'free'. This free-flow writing may capture the feel of this a little. Secondly, awakening is the seeing that there is nothing going anywhere, getting anything. There is no movement, no direction. Since these words are unplanned, just happening as they happen, the sense conveyed is one of meandering directionlessness, a quality usually regarded as undesirable in the vast majority of verbal discourses! Those books 'on nonduality' that are structured in seemingly progressive chapters, going from here to there, encourage the sense of movement; the sense that once a certain quantity of knowledge has been imparted, enlightenment will be closer. Reading this, I, this text, hope such illusions will not form so easily. This is really going nowhere...can you tell! My favourite book of this type (other than this one, naturally!!) is *All There Is* by Tony Parsons. A central aspect of that expression's effectiveness is the 'question and answer' nature of its form, which discourages the sense of 'going somewhere', of progression...since each question has its own agenda, its own enquiry, that often bears no relation to the previous question. There are limits to disabling this illusion of textual progression. For example, the title of a text inevitably triggers various expectations as to what the contents of that text may be; otherwise determining whether or not a book is 'the kind of thing I'm after' would be impossible.

18. Unease is belief in separation

Unease is belief in separation and 'the somebody'.

Shopping is so much smoother, lighter, friendlier

When it is seen that there is no one in the supermarket,

No critics, no judges, no aggressors to impress.

What The Sense Of 'Thought' Does

19. There is no such thing as 'thought'

'Thought' is feeling,

Sound and vision

And a sense that this feeling, sound, and vision

Are somehow one thing.

But this feeling of unity

Between these dissociated appearances

Is actually just one more singular, dissociated appearance.

For example,

It is imagined that there is some unified thing

That is the sound 'I',

A feeling or feelings of something like

'Presence', 'age', continuity', 'limitation', 'fragility',

And the image or images of something like

A blurry, limited, changeable, mortal 'object'

Or 'something'.

When the belief in there being connection

Between sound, image and feeling vanishes

It is seen that there is no such thing as 'thought'.

Notice this.

Notice that there is no 'thinking' going on right now.

There is this ink appearing, vision;

There is sound going on,

Sounding as these black ink forms are appearing;

There is feeling or taste too,

Perhaps a sense of structural collapse:

Refreshment, clarity, liberation?

And more images as well:

With the black squiggle 'green', the appearance of colour.

There is only the sensual.

The sensual is one experiencing

Called 'consciousness', 'being', or 'this'.

20. When doubt is known as 'it', awakening is doubtless.

Awakening is a blessedly certain actuality. Due to the plethora of confused information available on the subject, it often happens that the certainty is clouded over with doubt. However, with the recent and current climate generated by what has been named 'pure nonduality', it is increasingly likely that such doubt may be totally and terminally eradicated in a stroke. I see no reason why 'the glimpse', 'the transcendental experience', the temporary happening, cannot become a thing of the past: if it is realised that 'everything is it', including such feelings as disharmony, contraction, egotism and isolation, then there is no need for the sense of 'this not being it' to re-emerge. But this is all speculative. It is better to put energy into understanding the nature of the 'certainty', which is a fact.

Awakening is 'certain', beyond doubt, because it is the seeing that absolutely everything that occurs is purely, wholly, 'that' (oneness). Everything points to this, is this. Pain, irritation, aridity, self-centredness (as well as ecstasy, intoxication and love) – all of these are it and point vigorously to this fact. So how can there now be any sense of losing it? The sense of loss is it! Doubt is it! And then, what tends to happen is that certain appearances such as 'loss' and 'doubt' slowly, or quickly, dis-appear (although this is simply a tendency – it has nothing to do with what enlightenment is. The same goes for such things as identification, commendation and condemnation, blame and guilt). Realising this over and over again – 'Wow, that's it; and that, *and* that!' - can feel like an unstoppable 'multiplier effect', from nothing to infinity in a stroke.

21. There is no 'mind'

That which is called 'mind'

Is the sense of connectedness

And multiplicity.

Let this be explained.

There is colour.

'Mind' gets hold of this,

And translates 'redness above black circles'

Into 'car'.

Then there is the sound 'vroom'.

Again 'mind' creates 'car'.

'Mind' is the distorting spectacles

Through which 'sensation' appears as 'form'.

Through these lenses

The entire universe is born.

The reality of sensation so supple,

Untouched and untouchable,

Somehow translated

Into a vast agglomeration of 'objects'

(Some labelled 'subjects'):

'Mothers', 'selves', 'homes', 'nations', 'planets', 'Gods'…

'Mind'.

'Mind' itself is such an agglomeration,

objectification, misconception.

There is no mind.

Just supple nothingness,

Just this…

22. Object-subject demarcation is a fantasy

Here is a clear, accurate, immediate account of separation, awakening and nonduality. The separative perception is where a central demarcation, discrimination, division happens to the content of consciousness: some of the contents are labelled as 'me' (for example, thoughts, sensations, emotions and a particular body) while everything else is considered 'not me' (this book, these words, the room, the sky). This object/subject division provides and is the entire structure of the illusory 'material universe': if there is the belief that I am this body, or I am *in* this body, whether that be as a 'psychological ego' or a 'spiritual soul', then there is the sense of location, space and movement... I am 'here', and 'not me' is 'over there'. It makes reality appear as a thick, deep, solid, structural, material something.

Awakening is the seeing that the simple fact is - there is only consciousness, in which all happenings take place, *including* the demarcation, discrimination, division of happenings into subject/object. Thus, even the apparently separative impulse of identification, its seeming division, occurs within the wholly undivided, indivisible vision of pure consciousness. That is why, when awakening happens, it is paradoxically stated that awakeness, the nondualistic perspective, has always been the case.

Incidentally, and nothing more than an incidental, when both that which has been labelled 'the perceived', 'the object' and 'not me', and that which has been named 'the perceiver', 'the subject' and 'me', are seen as appearances in indivisible consciousness, the demarcation, discrimination, division impulse has a tendency to melt, collapse. And what happens to be felt a great deal, what tends to predominate attention often, is the presence of that consciousness that allows what is perceived to be. And that consciousness, or 'thisness', being beyond the sensate, is characterless, formless, timeless, unchanging.

23. A glimpse of God, then Godliness only

Meeting with Tony Parsons

'As she lay there dying,
Love poured from her eyes',
Said the lady at the meeting,
As love soared from her eyes…

And welled-up in the skies…
And plunged down from the ceiling…
And slapped into my lap…
And surged up from the seating…

Now all that's left is seeing;
One golden, molten site.
A sight that melts and welds 'me',
To all else, as light.

All there is is being,
So subtle, untouchably light.
A supple shimmering, a tingling,
Where once I lived my life.

Choice, Rhyme, Sex And Nonduality

24. There is no one 'in there'

Once you have read this,

Close your eyes,

And,

Seeing everything vanish,

Notice that the one, the someone,

Who appeared to close the eyes,

Is gone too.

This is the reality.

There is nothing...

Appearing as form.

25. Two largely irrelevant anecdotes

Today there is a sore throat and the general weakness and exhaustion of this. After eating a very large plate of bangers and mash this body collapsed upon the bed for what was hoped to be a rejuvenating period of relaxation that would enable this writing spell to come about, but what was actually expected to be an inevitable downward-spiralling into lethargy and slumber. What has actually happened is this. First it was noticed that, following the appearance of the decision to relax, a sense of 'a relaxer', who made this choice, came about, and that 'he' was now engaged in implementing this relaxation. Noticing this and the unreality of it, this ghostly sense vanished. Then, for what is an eternity, and for what may have been approximately twenty seconds, there was nothing at all. Total blankness, nothing. No sensation, no pressure, weight, of any kind. And then it was suddenly felt that there isn't so much tiredness after all – and on goes the computer, and here come these words!

This 'special experience' reminds me of my last aeroplane journey. In the past, virtually every time this body has flown there has been fairly intense earache throughout the plane's descent. This time, the first flight since awakening, a plan was hatched in which attention would be focused on the fact that really there is no going anywhere, that this plane is not really hundreds of miles in the air and travelling forwards at hundreds of miles an hour… in reality, there is only vacuousness, presence, awareness, sitting here, hanging here, nowhere, dead still. And, really, there is nothing called 'air pressure' that is changing, just as there is no plane and no descending.

Lo and behold, no earache came about on the plane's descent.

Of infinitely more importance and relevance than this incidental anecdote is the assertion that the incidental anecdote proves and means nothing. Earache is every bit as much the manifestation of nothingness as sitting in an aeroplane, concentrating on nothingness, and not getting earache is. It's just a story, without a moral. A non-fable.

26. Sex and social love offer glimpses of reality

Falling in love, in the human sense, most commonly between a man and a woman, is one of the most potent metaphors for this. One sees two bodies collapsing into each other, emotions both exhilarated and relaxed, all worries and thoughts, all deliberation - the inventing of past and future, of time - just vanishing in the light of love.

27. Rhyme is synonymous with desire, the impulse to repeat

Rhyme is the same kind of slime sex is.

It is compulsion, addiction.

Addiction is fine,

Sex is fine,

Rhyme is fine -

But these 'notices', by and large, avoid such things.

Rhyme is most appropriate for the conveyance of *psychology*.

Psychology is where a certain sensate experience happens,

Is replicated mentally,

And then this replica is used to reconstruct 'the experience'

All over again,

And again

And again.

Rhyme embodies this process:

It is an addiction to

The pleasurable experience of repetitive sound-patterning.

Rhyme feels less appropriate in the majority of these 'notices'

As these notices are concerned

With pointing out oneness directly,

Immediately,

Telegraphically.

Once something gets stuck in the brain,

Replicated as thought,

It becomes difficult to look beyond that replica

And simply see.

When rhyme is used here

It is usually for the purpose of mnemonics.

As in

'I am not a conscious man;

Consciousness is what I am.'

Although this is, of course, a 'sticking in the mind'

It largely resists 'forming',

Taking shape,

As 'consciousness'

Is a word that tends not to produce much of a sensory response.

(This is just as well,

As consciousness is unimaginable.)

28. Seeing there is no choice, is freedom from guilt (an email)

I want to try to avoid concepts and opinions and arguments in this paragraph – like the plague. So this is my experience of 'the relief' I talked about. I finally absorbed a message I had been forever skipping over; that there is no choice, no one there to choose. The feeling was of 23 years of guilt, fear, struggle, awkwardness, all that sort of thing, being wiped clean in an instant. I felt completely assured – that I had never done a single thing wrong, that I could never get anything wrong in the future, that there was no 'me' capable of this; and suddenly there was love, and absence of fear and a freedom that felt like it was almost too much, overbalancing. It also made everything so simple because, yes, there was just 'this'. When I had been meditatively 'focusing' (I know that's the wrong word) on 'the here and now', it had sometimes produced lovely blissful states, but there was also a sense that I could slip out of this, 'fall back', or whatever. But now there is no possibility of this, no way of getting anything wrong.

29. Rhyme, lust and addiction are the same (immaculate impulse)

Perhaps a timely sex-interlude is called for? It calls itself. Have a look at these:

This is what is meant by 'Catchy',
Movement which captures a cat completely;
The way she curves, holds the he,
As she stalks, catwalks, so felinely.

Her pout, doubtless directed at me,
Is a conscious scratch; these claws of the catty
Shall always capture me – here, do you see?
Of course her neck-tag names her 'Catchy'.

She latches herself to the end of this pen,
Yet coils so slippery, she goes on eluding me,
There is nothing so catchy as poetry
When the lines rhyme as obsessive as these.

'Rhyme Addiction', is this disease,
The same affliction, as sex, or sneezin';
It is that which goes on pulling me,
As in the chorus of pop-ditties.

And here we see it perfectly.
That which is 'Catchy', in all her majesty:
White trash Britney, black cat Beyonce,
Rhyming and writhing as one weave.

So, readers, basically,
It all boils down to titillating titties:
There is no such thing as 'a she', actually,
But charming curves, *are here*, doubtlessly.

30. There is no choice, just impulses like 'sex'

Willy-nilly

Sex compels,
Impels like nothing else;
Sex dwells in the pulling of this pen.
Rhyme is the same kind of slime sex is,
That same stickiness,
So say, 'sex spells':

Sex sticks in the words 'flesh' and 'lust'
And 'breasts' and 'legs' and 'sex' and such.

Believe some 'I' lies behind these lines?
Some 'blob' in the skies?
Some 'thing' behind eyes?

Just throbs behind flies
And inside her thighs,
Entwined in these rhymes,
That lie in these lines;

This writer, male,
His poem, female,
Nothing but the tempting tell of a tale.

And then... then...
- *Yes, you know when!* -
Like nothing else
Wet sex repels,

And nothing is my will.

31. Nonduality and sex energise (this text); most texts striptease

A quick note. The only two subjects this text traverses, it can be seen, are nonduality and sex. Nothing else rouses the sufficient degree of energy for sustained textual output here. Nondualistic expression gestures (though note that it is impossible to gesture towards what is everywhere and everything) to what is eternal, indefatigable, and in this, the body involved with moving fingers, pressing keys, notices this tireless freshness and feels light and vitalised. The infinite is eternal self-sustenance. Not altogether unalike is the subject 'sex', which, when fixed on by the mind, gives rise to a feverish energy that fuels the production of many an obscene poem...as you and I have witnessed! In a way, though we are on shaky ground here, one might conceptualise 'sex' as lying at the very crotch of reality: it is infinite energy pouring into the apparent creation of multiplicity...which then, in orgasm, melts back into the delicious, golden-syrupy bliss of oneness, the infinite primeval soup, which, at the same time, represents new output, new life. Really, though, there is no 'oneness' separate from any 'manifestation of multiplicity', joined by any 'crotch'. There is only oneness.

Talking of sex and crotches, it is not irrelevant to note that the vast majority of literary texts operate as stripteases. The title, the front cover, and the opening lines and chapters of a text are a seduction attempt, with the end of soliciting readership. Something is hinted at, half revealed, just like the stripper with her suggestive clothes and gestures, the full revelation of which is postponed until the delicious climax of the text, where an orgasmic satisfaction of some kind is finally administered. The murderer is found out, the hero and heroine finally understand each other and get it together...everybody dies! So texts, the vast majority of them, are fundamentally engaged in setting up readership hopes, fears, anticipations, teasing the reader through stimulating suggestion and suspension, before stripping its secret, fulfilling its promise. What this engenders is the generation of a world of time, a sense that 'I am here, at the beginning of this book' and 'there is a future before me, in which I will ascertain something, attain something, in which this beginning, and my newfound desire, shall be fulfilled'.

This text draws attention to this because, with a few playful exceptions, *this text* is fundamentally engaged in taking one big fat mallet to the textual time machine. The stripper has been sacked, or rather, never employed. She does not exist here. This destruction of time, or rather the non-creation of it, is achieved or attempted through a variety of literary methods, namely sporadic changes of subject and a general pervading meandering directionless...where nothing seems to happen go anywhere, get anything...have you noticed?! Oh yes, and pointless repetition too. As the truth is, there is no such thing as time, or space for that matter, disorientation, dislocation, is the aim here. There is only this, which never moves, which is infinite and placeless. Look: in the erotic novel, there are bodies entwining, lives entangling, stories ravelling, revelling, the revealing of colours, forms and sounds...you can see all this now, reading this, and yet there is only the appearance of this, and the appearance of these tricksy black squiggles, in a consciousness that is omnipresent and changeless.

As a substitute for the allure of the gratifying stripper and his or her teasing act, this text, as you may have noticed, so that someone, somewhere, might just read it, administers, periodically, copious dollops of crude, wholly gratuitous sex. There is more to this than just 'reader (and writer) sustenance' though. One of the fallacies propagated by some so-called teachers of nonduality is that awakening engenders a certain natural celibacy or asexuality. Awakening, remember, is purely and wholly the seeing that *everything that is* – sex, celibacy, Al Qaeda – is oneness, awareness, light. So there are no behavioural conditions. Yes, there may be resultant characteristic tendencies: for example, if there is a knowing that nobody wrote and published a crude, thoroughly un-English poem called 'Willy-Nilly', it is possible that less embarrassment will happen; as compared to where the belief 'I wrote this poem and anyone else will see it over my dead body' is present. But this is not a direct function of awakening and is only a possibility.

With regards to sex, I have so far noticed little or no change in this organism's sexual activity, subsequent to realisation. It periodically craves arousal and orgasm, and afterwards, the craving is not there...until it is there again! All very normal I feel. And this very natural, biological patterning, this periodic appearance and disappearance of sexual desire, I have attempted to convey in this text, through the similarly periodic appearance of the subject in the narrative. Its sudden, sporadic coming-and-going, moreover, reflects the uncontrollability of the sexual – that it 'just happens'. As such, it is a very potent pointer to the nature of reality, the fact that there is no power, no directive, just uncontrolled happenings. For example, a sense of 'will' may happen, the idea that there is a somebody in charge of something, some directive power, but this sense just happens, or doesn't, and reflects only the presence of a fundamental misconstruction. The term 'willy-nilly', meaning 'whether one likes it or not', is, says the OED, a 'later spelling of *will I, nill I,* I am willing, I am unwilling'. 'Willy-nilly', then, is an excellent term for how reality is: there is no will, no centre, no cause and effect. This is purely willy-nilly.

All There Is, Is Choice-less Awareness

32. What you are, what is, is indivisible awareness

It has now occurred that the playfulness of preceding passages could do with being followed, now, by a more clear, sober, precise discourse. Textual 'playfulness' has the function of performing that which is creation always and everywhere, nothingness appearing as 'thingness', all manner of things, objects, identities, stories...all that appears. So it has its place in such as book as this. But now for the sober bit.

The simplest way I, this text, can think of stating the essential expression of this text is as follows. It is observed that there are certain things that get labelled as 'me' and other things, all the rest, that get labelled as 'not me'. Looking at this, it can be seen that this labelling, and the division it represents, are not primary, not fundamental. They are added, imposed. And what they are added to, it can be seen, is that which sees this imposed dividing and labelling. That which sees this, that which is fundamental, is without character, form, quality – as character, form, quality are always seen, witnessed, of the senses. So what you are is that in which everything appears, including division and labelling, variety and movement, birth and death. So what you are, what really is, is immortal, is immortality.

33. 'Author' and 'narrator' are pure fictions

Notice that there is no one here

Inviting you to notice that there is no one here.

'The author' and 'the narrator'

Are pure fictions.

This is just ink.

This is just a notice.

34. You are pure fiction

Do you believe that 'you' are 'over there',

Reading 'this page' that is 'over here'?

Notice that this sense of location,

Of an 'over there' and 'over here',

Is registered, witnessed or felt by something.

That 'something' is pre-existent.

It is what you really are.

It is not located anywhere:

All sense of space and time arise within it.

It is therefore timeless and placeless.

35. Nonduality says nothing

One of the many ways of spotting a misleading teaching is by asking whether or not there seems to be some kind of agenda or movement, like a political or ethical movement, involved in it. An example of this would be where a message is put out that 'one should desire the enlightenment of as many people as possible', that 'that would be better'. Clarity reveals that perfection, the immaculate, is already totally present. It is as redolently, radiantly present in conflict, suffering and the belief in separation, as it is in the seeing that there is only oneness. Oneness is obviously everything. Of course, this extends wholeheartedly to the kind of change-advocating teaching being discussed, this is totally and only oneness advocating change, but what is revealed is the confusion (yes, the divine confusion, the immaculate misconception) of that expression. Human appearances desiring changes to the appearance is perfectly natural and healthy, before and after awakening. The body naturally dislikes flu and a stubbed toe and enjoys, for example, a tasty roast, an all-over body massage and meditation. But this is an entirely separate issue to that of the absolute, of that which is always and everywhere absolutely the case, and to associate the two is unhelpfully confusing.

My hunch is that the kind of message that advocates change, whether it be 'towards a more harmonious planet' or 'in the direction of a stiller mind', derives from a love of unity. It is a love so strong, it is allowed to compromise the expression of *unicity*. This kind of compromised message is most commonly expressed, perhaps always, in a setting keen on promoting the supposed virtues of 'the spiritual community' and/or 'spiritual independence and solitude'. The concern here is with 'human unity' – a number of 'human units' uniting to form a larger unit called something like 'a sangha' or simply 'a group', or a single 'human unit' hermetically isolating himself in the pursuit of some confused concept such as 'spiritual autonomy', in which there is supposed to be the becoming of a completed unit, a perfect individual unity.

My guess is that when certain nobodies awaken to unicity there remains a certain personal fondness and attachment to the kind of social existence they may have enjoyed for many years; all that hugging, hymn-singing, guitar strumming, orgy-having… And understandably so! So they naturally set up a similar sort of community in the hope of continuing this pleasurable (through asceticism and the exhilarating sense of achievement it can bestow, as much as through direct sensual Epicureanism), special kind of existence. And there is absolutely nothing wrong with this. Enjoyment is fine…enjoyment is enjoyment. But sometimes, in order that the community be created and sustained, it is suggested, implicitly or explicitly, that the community and the communion that can take place within it are somehow 'sacred', beneficial to awakening. This is not so. This is a lie. There is no relationship between awakening and unity, community or global harmony; or at least the same relationship as awakening has to disunity and world war. How can there be any relationship where the absolute is concerned? The absolute is everything; it has no relations. No setting, no practice, no ethics can bring can bring anyone a single step closer to what they already are, what is already, Absolutely, the case.

36. On 'pausing' and 'no one to choose' (an email)

Dear Sam,

I hope this will be the letter I have been promising both you and me. The only thing that possibly stands in the way is that it is now 12.20am and I'm a little weary, so we shall see if I can last the distance. I'm hoping that this situation will force me to consider what I am saying very clearly and precisely, to avoid tiring ramble, although in saying this, I am already failing.

There will be two parts to this, the first a lot easier than the second. Sam, one recommendation I have, based on recent rather ferocious experiences of my own, is that if you ever have strongly 'negative' feelings, then a very helpful thing is to simply close your eyes and watch what is happening, in terms of sensation in particular. My own problem was a very tight twisting or clenching in my stomach and around my heart - it was this kind of sensation that for whatever reason prompted those suicidal thoughts - which I think became compounded by an urge on my part to squeeze this tighter and tighter, as if somehow trying to drill through it, to reach a point where it vanished (perhaps something to do with some strange, unhelpful beliefs I had about purgation and enlightenment).

One day the clutching was so strong, it finally made me overcome my shyness of phoning up one of the guys I used to visit in London - Roger. He recommended simply this 'pausing' I described above; he said something like 'It restores natural balance and functioning'. He would very definitely not call it 'meditation', because with meditation there is usually a sense of going somewhere... 'inwards', or 'somewhere more still and energized', or, paradoxically, 'the-here-and-now'. With this 'pausing' everything is allowed, everything is it. If, for example, there's a sense of 'increased stillness' or of 'moving inwards', that's fine, but equally, so are senses of 'chaos', 'confusion', and 'trying to get somewhere'.

With this specific instance of pausing the emotional clenching immediately began to ease and unclench. It started off as a dense, pressurized mass, and then, throughout the next few days, it gradually uncoiled like a snake, with a sense of upward movement, until it dispersed, leaving a tender feeling much like bruising. I think this was a very marked example, though, and everyone is different. What might happen, though, is that when these feelings soften a little, whether they be anger, or chronic frustration, loathing, disgust, jealousy, guilt, the thoughts and impulses in your mind may alter; and usually I find the kind of ideas going on in this softer, more balanced, 'restored', 'natural' state are far more helpful to me. One last thing about this: you can't get it wrong. If the thoughts 'I don't get this', or 'This isn't working' happen, for example, then that is what is happening, that is what is. That is the content of the 'pausing'. Even if there is the impulse to try and get rid of the feeling, then that is simply 'what is'.

I hope that's helpful, Sam; please get in touch if you have any doubts or queries about it.

This second part is harder to communicate; my body just produced an extra wave of tiredness to tempt me to give up without trying! Let me try. God, I already feel defeated! I'll just go about it directly. I now feel one hundred per cent certain that there is nothing I can do to influence my life in any way, or that actually I have ever managed this, because I have seen that there is no such person there. Before there was the thought 'There is someone in here'; now there is no such thought. Not that this makes it anymore believable, but I am also 100% sure that this assertion will never change, because I know it and see it.

This sounds terribly dogmatic, but there we are. It is so clear and obvious to me... I don't know what else to say. So my 'advice' has to be: you have absolutely no control over whether you are going to stay in Shanghai, come back to England, feel happy or unhappy, or whether you are cruel to somebody or friendly to them. But somehow, when it is seen that there is no one there to do any of these things, there is a certain relief, smoothness, playfulness and contentment. You can't go wrong, you have never gone wrong, you can never 'do well' in the world, or fail. It is completely hopeless.

While there is the belief that there is a 'you' who can 'make or break' 'your life' there is a continuous sense of struggle, dissatisfaction, a not quite living up to expectations or where you want to be. It's a nagging or itching or sense of 'not-quite-right-ness'.

Maybe it's more helpful for me to come at it from my own experience. At some point (around a month back?), this message that there is no one with any choice finally began to sink in. It wasn't something I could argue cerebrally, but it just seemed to be accepted on some level, and this produced very tangible and deep-feeling senses of relief, self-acceptance and dissolution of all guilt and sense of responsibility. For a while, I didn't quite 'get it', because I thought this meant I had to wait until things happened; that, for example, 'actively seeking employment through apparently wielding my will' was 'going against' this. However, it is now clear that this (seemingly choosing a job, etc) is every bit this choice-less happening, nothing can be outside of this. Another way of putting this, which has also helped 'make the penny drop' with me, is that 'there is only oneness, nothing can be outside of it'. The kind of teachings I used to be into definitely disabled this aspect, because, for me at least, there was always the sense that one practice (eg meditation) was more worthwhile, more the act of divinity, oneness, than another (eg masturbation, being cruel to one's girlfriend, watching *Neighbours*, pouring scolding water over one's friend and housemate, etc). But really, if oneness is a fact, then it can't be more here than there. Whenever the feeling 'I am going wrong', 'I am missing the boat', or, in my case, 'doing something that is taking me away from this enlightenment I have believed in' happens, a quick adjustment (not a belief) makes me realise that this is *just oneness* thinking it is 'going wrong', *oneness* thinking it is 'missing the boat': and then there is no 'going wrong', or anywhere - there is just oneness/presence/being/awareness happening...appearing to be going somewhere, appearing to be doing something.

I have a horrible feeling this hasn't communicated at all. If any of it has resonated, that's great, but there's nothing I or you can do about it unfortunately. Please let me know what, if any, has been the response. Does it piss you off? I remember talking to a friend about this kind of thing once and he got absolutely livid and would have refused to let me enter his house if I hadn't made him feel absurd for doing that.

I should add that something permanent certainly seems to have clicked with me, Sam, and I can't see how it can be anything other than permanent. I see that everything in oneness, including 'oneness ego-ing', 'oneness thinking it is a separate individual', 'oneness thinking it isn't oneness', oneness (apparently) killing people (oneness). Seriously Sam, I watched a programme about Saddam Hussein and felt waves of love and bliss at killers and killings, which to any normally educated human being would seem warped or wrong!

Incidentally, meditation certainly tends to generate the sense 'This isn't it', because there can be these delicious ecstatic highs, and then, when this is gone, there is the belief 'I have lost it' or 'This isn't it' – 'It needs to come back again'. This is totally mistaken though; there's just oneness (however ordinary it feels).

That's enough; this has either rung a bell or it hasn't. I hope it at least doesn't irritate you.

I must get some shut-eye!

Lots of love Sam,

Guy

37. There is no 'choice' whatsoever

Do you think that you are choosing to read this?

If anything,

It is these words that are grabbing your attention.

You don't know what words are here

And what they have to say

Until you read them,

So how can you make any choice

About whether to read them or not?

Even if you agree with this

You may believe you have the power to choose

Whether or not to continue reading.

'The first bit is boring, so the chances are – so is the rest of it.'

Actually,

You cannot even choose this: there is no such thing as 'choice'.

Notice that continued reading either happens

Or it doesn't.

Continued reading may have followed the thought

'I think I will continue reading'

But that is just something else that happened,

Another uncontrollable event.

This is just happening.

There is no choice and no responsibility.

When this is seen

Guilt and blame dissolve as misconceptions.

Then there is freedom,

Redemption,

Eternal salvation.

And there is absolute forgiveness of everything and everyone.

This is love.

There Is No Such Thing As 'A Woman'

38. Dramatising the nothingness of self and the force of libido

More sex everybody! Here we go:

A beautiful girl lifts up my head,
A beautiful girl pulls me out of bed,
She beckons me over, into her net,
A beautiful girl leaves me hot and wet.

Then off the computer I get.
A glass of water, and I am set,
And out of the house I head.

A beautiful girl takes me out and about,
A beautiful girl sets me on the lookout,
A short skirt, a pert pout,
The beautiful girl from the advert mounts,
At every corner she is ready to pounce,
Her simulation, her stimulation
Is womanhood, every ounce.

A beautiful girl calls me back to the house,
She cooks my dinner, I warm the couch;
A beautiful girl pulls me into bed,
Turns out the light, enough said.

39. There is no such thing as 'a woman'

The claim that a two-dimensional photographic image of 'a beautiful girl' or at least 'a female body' 'is womanhood, every ounce' may to seem to some a ridiculous and insulting sentiment. This is the misconception. 'Womanhood' is the misconception. Identity, individuality is the misunderstanding. Virtually the whole of that appearance labelled 'human society' occupies itself with 'bigging itself up', that is to say, feverishly propagating the belief that there is such a thing as selfhood, a me and a you, and that these 'selves' are the most important, big and solid things there are. Feminism busies itself with projecting the idea of 'the woman', psychoanalysis with 'the ego' and 'the unconscious', religion with 'the soul', politicians with 'the free-will' of 'one man, one vote'. There is no such thing as selfhood.

Imagine that what you have labelled 'a woman' is standing before you, right now. There are colours – say, pervasively pink, if that colour is being worn or perhaps nothing worn – there is movement, there may be a sound along the lines of 'Oi! Stop drooling at me, punk!' or 'I'm not a lesbian you know' or 'Yes I am, big girl'. Perhaps the image is getting bigger and now there is sensation arising – softness, roundness, breath, thrills of energy, or disgust perhaps! But where in all of this sumptuousness or repulsiveness is there 'a woman'? Or a 'you' for that matter, receiving the attention? See what the mind does? It creates these solid, incredibly convincing images, imaginings, that are total phantoms, mirages. Everything is far more liquid, light, ungraspable than this. In fact again and again there is nothing there – just nothing presenting itself. And this is the joy of writing poetry. One (oneness) delighting in the radical, free game of assuming whatever identity it desires, fearlessly spouting provocative bravado about a billboard being 'womanhood, every ounce'! 'The beautiful girl from the advert' weighs not an 'ounce', she is but a visual image; but so does and is that which you call 'a woman'. There is no such thing. And then the whole concept of 'Women's Liberation' is seen as comically oxymoronic. Woman can never be liberated: woman is enslaved to be woman. Freedom is the seeing that identity is nothing, there is no one, no woman, and then all just happens, appears, like a mighty firework display in the eyes of an infant: spontaneous arising as opposed to determined, planned, responsible action.

One important appendage to this: I am not saying that, for example, movements to diminish abusive and enslaving behaviour are 'comically oxymoronic': it is a thoroughly natural, healthy and intelligent bodily and emotional response to desire the lessening of pain and misery. What is being said here is that it is the forming of definition, of identity, that is the cause of all bondage, whether that be the defining of 'woman' as a subhuman, inferior something, or as an equal, independent, unique somebody, or even as superior, more sensitive, empathic, better-at-multitasking-and-exams-than-the-boys. However definition is formed, it is static, and therefore imprisoning; abstract, and so obstructive to the seeing of the ungraspable, ineffable, incomparable liquidity of 'what is'.

Back to the poem, the concept and indeed the term 'simulation' is very much associated with that contemporary something called 'the postmodern'. One activity of the postmodern has been to question the hierarchical demarcation of 'the real', e.g. 'Guy Smith', from 'the representation', e.g. a painting of Guy Smith. Likewise, the closing phrase of the poem, 'enough said', might be called 'postmodern' in that it embodies an irresolvable ambiguity. What, how much, is 'enough'? In this case it seems that 'enough' means 'enough to make a poem in which not enough has been said to know exactly what is going on'. Does this final phrase represent the rather belated gesture of sanctifying the intimate, the narrator making love to his woman in the dark, with privacy? Perhaps they are just going straight off to sleep, or simply turning the lights out. Perhaps it is broad daylight! Perhaps there isn't really any such 'real woman' present in the poem at all: perhaps all the references to 'a beautiful girl' are purely phantasmic mental projections generated by and fuelling the male sex-drive and the narrator's movements in the poem? After all, that is exactly what drives the poem into existence, what fuels its presence, its being.

The lovely thing about all this semantic openness is that it represents, simulates or rather *is* exactly how life really is. One of the differences between postmodern discourse and nondualistic expression is that the former falsely interprets this to be a state of terrifying existential uncertainty and disorientation, what it calls 'undecidability'. In the case of 'womanhood' considered above, for example, the postmodern might revel and wallow in an endless questioning of 'what is a woman?', 'where is the woman?' and so on. In contrast, nonduality sees with crystal-clarity and concrete-certainty that there is no woman anywhere, womanhood is a misconception. There are no objects in reality: reality is no-thing appearing.

40. Desire and belief in 'the other' are oneness, as all is (an email)

Hi Phil,

I want to write to you at this moment, but, like everything else I begin today, as soon as I get there, I have no interest. You know that experience when life is continually believed to be somewhere else? First it was 'finishing work' (while working), then it was 'being at home in front of the cricket' (while walking home), then it was 'falling asleep to build up energy "to how it should be" (while watching the cricket). And all of this happened against the backdrop of thinking I should be out in the sun, because that's more healthy, because it'll make me look all brown, blonde, blue-eyed and attractive to women, and it might be rainy tomorrow.

All of this has inspired one nice reflective bit of clarity though. It is clear that prior to awakening I would definitely have believed that all of this yearning for otherness was very dualistic and unenlightened. (Incidentally, I would also have believed in the extinction of this impulse by, say, meditation or 'not being a slave to my desires', 'leaving these chocolate biscuits next to me alone'. But actually, of course, this activity is nothing but a function of this very yearning for elsewhereness, the wish to be 'somewhere still, a place beyond desire'.) But the fact is, the fact that is so clear and obvious now and which makes this all so simple, that all of this, everything, including all desire, including the desire for desirelessness, is the presence, oneness, that is absolutely unmoving, desireless.

Remembering and seeing this is a kind of permissiveness and love for the processes - making them playful. And at other times this somehow gets in amongst all the dry striving and softens it, melts it.

One very annoying thing Phil. I have found it impossible to open your jam-jar. Not only is it sealed so hard it is even a match for Guru Guy here - the lid is serrated. I have tried pouring hot water on the lid and also using a cloth to dampen the sharp bits, but all in vain.

I guess that's it in a nutshell (or rather a jam-jar). Guy has spent all day trying to get into the jam-jar, when really there is no jam. 'What is' is redness and the idea of sweetness... and nothing else.

41. 'A woman' is an object; there is no such thing as 'an object'

How can 'a woman' be liberated?
A woman is 'an object'.
An object is limited,
Imprisoned by what it is.

How can 'a subject' be free?
A subject is 'subjected'.
Determined by nature and nurture only,
A puppet is all it can be.

And is a puppet really a being?
Of course it isn't really.
Lips move, sounds sound,
But nowhere is 'a someone' found.

And this is liberation!
Seeing I am but impersonation,
Free I am of this mimicry,
This inhibiting pretence of 'me'.

42. Nonduality is fanatically political, and absolutely apolitical

Nonduality has nothing to say about politics, morality, judgement and so on. All of these things are made of this nonduality that is, yes, amoral, but an amorality that is morality as well as amorality. This sounds daft, but it is absolutely true. What is meant is that nonduality is everywhere and everything and as such is as accepting of morality, whether that be nazism, monarchy, capitalism, communism, as it is of amorality. It is an absence of hierarchy that totally embraces hierarchy. It is an absence of movement that totally embraces all movements. It *does not* say that 'amorality' and 'nonjudgementalness' are higher or better than morality and judgement. It is silent on all these subjects, and also it is in and *is* the vigorous speech of all the various proponents of each and every point of view.

Although I know nothing of the specifics I have heard that communism in China attempted to exhibit Lao Tzu's *Tao Te Ching* as a manifesto that recommends communism. I will briefly follow through an argument that supports an equating of nonduality and communism and then demonstrate the falseness of this premise by presenting the equally convincing argument that nonduality is capitalistic.

So, one might say that communism is the political orientation of nonduality because in the former 'the individual' must share all his possessions, in effect he has both no possessions and all possessions, and in nonduality it is seen that there is no ownership, no owner and no owned. On the other hand, one might say that capitalism is the political orientation of nonduality because, when there is nonduality, it is seen that everything is immaculate as it is and that the beggar is no less wealthy than the king. So the hierarchy is every bit as embraced as the commune, by something that is totally beyond, and totally in, both.

43. Life is ventriloquism, without ventriloquist

In ventriloquism

A puppet appears to speak,

But doesn't.

In a pop video

Some bodies seem to sing,

But don't.

It is mimicking.

It is lip-synching.

Even on radio

Bodies are seen,

Persons imagined

Behind the singing.

They are not there;

There is nothing there.

In oration

A body appears to orate.

What actually happens

Is the movement of lips

And the sounding of sound:

Sound isn't made by any body;

Lips aren't operated by 'a somebody'.

Here, now, these sounds appear

These forms are here

These black squiggles.

But no body is saying them,

No one wrote them –

It's the ventriloquism

Of no one.

44. Depression is 'infinite fulfilment' manifesting as depression

Bodily illness, just your basic fluey symptoms, sore-throat and general lethargy in particular, have been here for an unusually long time, and, waking up this morning, it was evident that this longevity is taking a psychological toll: a certain sullenness or gloominess, what might be termed 'mild depression'. Enlightenment is not about being in impregnable states of delirious ecstasy or good spirits. It has nothing to do with any change or specified order in what appears, in life, it is solely about seeing *sub specie aeternitatis*, 'from the perspective of eternity' (as that expression commonly labelled 'Baruch Spinoza' and 'a Dutch philosopher' describes it). Actually, this is the only seeing there can be: everything that happens registers in a seeing or knowingness that is obviously beyond what is seen and known, that is beyond space and time and is therefore 'the perspective of eternity'. But there is a point when this seeing is re-cognized, and this does have a certain impact. This is what is called 'awakening'. When it seen, for example, that a mood or state of depression has manifested, this is known purely as a certain feeling, a specific arrangement of energy, rather than, say, something 'wrong', an indication that 'my life needs a radical overhaul, that I need a new woman, a more expensive reflexologist, to give up red meat' or that 'I am a fundamentally fucked-up loser'. Yes, a healthier diet, for example, might diminish the probabilities of bodily illnesses, and hence the particular emotional gloominess felt this morning, and that is fine, a perfectly reasonable and intelligent thing to do, but what is seen, from the perspective of eternity, is that depression is OK, it need not be got rid of; it arises, is tasted, felt, and disappears again, and that's fine. Divine, in fact.

45. Art is oneness (as all is), and is effulgent of that

Some so-called 'nondualists' claim or imply that art, and certain kinds of art, are more oneness, more sacred, than other things, than science, for example. This is pure ignorance: the absolute is obviously *absolutely* everywhere, in everything, and cannot be more 'here' than 'there'. However, one might say that art is representative, or reflective or like a microcosm (although this is wrong), of the nature of oneness, in a way that science (for example) isn't. Being involved in a certain movement, a process, known as 'reasoning', science perpetually translates: it says 'This is so *because of* something else'. Everything is determined, caused, by something prior to it. (It should be noted here that this apparent process is every bit as much oneness as all else). In contrast, art, or at least what is called 'good art', simply presents itself, as it is. It is not about process or translation; art exists for no reason other than its own existence. Science is 'the how'; art is 'the what'. And as such, art reflects the nature of 'reality', because reality is actually going nowhere, there is really no time at all. One might also distinguish 'good art' from 'consumer or popular art' by this very contrast of process and stillness. The whole energy of 'consumer art' – say, Stephen King, Harry Potter – is invested in the solicitation of a desire that is suspended in a seductive manner until the end of the book, so the reader reads not for the present but for the future. In 'good art', it is the 'what is present now' that is the emphasis, the immediate beauty or power of the art's very fabric, the colour, the image, the sound. It is sensate reality at its most sensitive, sensuous and sensual.

Absolute
Contentment
Is Not A Possibility:
It *Is* Reality

46. 'The in-control individual' and 'the subjected subject' are fictions

Many different names have been given to this phantom – 'the self'. One popular name has been 'the individual'. Derived from the Latin *individuus*, meaning 'undivided' or 'not divisible', the word 'individual' may be seen to represent the view that selfhood is autonomous, free, totally conscious, and 'in control'. Perhaps stemming most influentially from Sigmund Freud's psychoanalytic account of the unconscious, more recent thought, particularly that which is labelled 'the postmodern', has tended to prefer the term 'the human subject', which promotes the sense that 'the self' is primarily or wholly a thing of subjugation. It is subjected to, the subject of, uncontrollable, controlling influences of genetics and conditioning, much of which is unconscious, unseen, and therefore impossible to challenge or combat (and even if it were, that which challenged it, say, 'the conscious mind', is itself purely a creation of conditions beyond itself). All of this is very fascinating and endlessly complex, which the mind loves, but the simple fact that there is no selfhood instantly vaporises the whole of this theoretical mire. No one is subject to anything. No one is in control of anything. There is no influence and nothing to be influenced. Look: where is this somebody supposed to be a victor or victim, an individual or subject? There is only consciousness, in which this book-reading is being staged. Yes, things happen, but to a nothingness that is without character.

47. Nonduality is logical and empirical

The mind confronted with the message of nonduality

Finds itself in a quandary.

On the one hand what is being said sounds ludicrous.

What do you mean there is no world out there?

I *was* born on this date!

My Mum *is* real!

I *am* a real somebody!!

On the other hand, what nonduality says

Is wholly logical and empirical.

It is seen that nothing lasts

Or remains the same for even an instant.

It is known that what is labelled 'the real world'

Is so feeble it collapses roughly once or more a day

In what is known as 'sleep'.

And, deep down, it is felt beyond doubt

That there is nobody.

The pain of loneliness,

The tender sensing of shallowness and phoniness

Is this realisation calling itself.

48. I am loved (written days after awakening)

Out in the morning air,
Hanging out washing for Granny,
When suddenly I am aware:
This is all happening for me!

The bird in the tree
Sings 'attention attention!
Guy I love thee…
Marry me!'

The grass glaring green
With glorious envy
Strokes my feet
And holds me…

The blue in the sky,
Bright dyes of the cloths,
The great bombing fly
And sleeping moth;

The fondling grass green,
The shyer soft moss,
The breeze that touches,
The hair that wafts…

And all for me,
All calling me,
In love with me,
Absolutely!

And none playing hard to get!

Even the girl
I imagine in a whirl,
Her patchwork skirt

Fanning free above knees,
And feet flat in the dirt.

Her gaze down there,
Ignoring me,
As if I weren't here…

And yet she flirts!
She loves me totally!
Her playing hard to get
Is yet

The declaration of adoration,
A violent expression of adulation –

I am loved!
I am loved!
I am loved!

49. The seeing of oneness can be the most uncanny of feelings

Sometimes hearing this sort of message can lead to a response of trepidation. One imagines a looming figure behind these words who is dauntingly powerful, resolute, knowledgeable, superior. A someone altogether different from yourself. I know that feeling very well. I would like to tell you that this strange figure appearing here, this disembodied voice talking to you now, or that gaunt, simian, slow, shy figure that might one day stand before you at a 'meeting with Guy Smith', is nothing but you yourself. He is not different at all. He is more than your best friend, your mother or your lover...I am you, just as those familiar old hands holding this book are you. Relax – I am your body, I am your pet dog, I am your warm, safe house, I am your reflection in the mirror...I am so close to you I am the same as you.

There is an essay entitled *The Uncanny*, usually attributed to an imagined something called 'Sigmund Freud', which basically states that an uncanny experience is one in which something that is 'secretly known' happens. For example, a man's first experience of sex proves to be a disturbing, disenchanting experience, miles away from the soft-focus erotic fantasies he has dreamed up prior to and about intercourse. Naked in the arms of a woman, seeing and feeling a womb, suddenly there is terror, shaking, shame, disgust. Lying dormant in the unconscious lie all manner of traumatic memories of birth and infancy...now suddenly they are evoked... yet so traumatic were they, they have been repressed beyond recognition. The strange paralysing terror of the experience, then, lies in the secret recognition of something so traumatic it has been repressed beyond conscious recollection. 'I *know* this; this is déjà vu' screams something somewhere in the psyche, yet this only makes what is believed to be a wholly new experience all the more strange, uncanny.

Faced with a text or oral discourse that induces a heightened awareness of what really is, what you really are, just this sense of the uncanny can emerge. 'I *know* this...I *remember* this', something can suddenly say, 'I know *you*'. In this context, it is little wonder that the apparent communicator suddenly appears as a disturbing, haunting presence. There is something overwhelmingly familiar about what is being said and what is going on, yet, in terms of the life-story, you have never seen this person before, never come across the words he or she is saying nor the kind of setting in which they are being said. Peculiar – and very powerfully so.

This must be the most uncanny experience possible. The recognition of what is being said is so incredibly potent, unbearably so, because it has been seen, has been the case, all the time, every single moment of your life over and over and over... And yet the mind is frantically desperate to rally against it: 'How can this be so?' it says, 'It *is* true that I *am* a person...All of those memories *are* real...I *did* do this, I *did* achieve that...That person *did* and *does* love me and *is* at home this very minute cooking my Sunday roast!' It is a ferocious melting-pot – in which faces bend, memories swim, and belief-structures career and crash-down to ashes. And this consciousness, the fire in which it all dances, reveals itself as a torrent too ragged, too choppy, too wild for words...nothing to hold onto, no foothold, no ground... absolute raw freedom. And then, finally, is the deep, tranquil 'ah'. Cool breezes across tropical beaches, coral reefs in turquoise seas...cocktails in hand, parasols, palms and bare soles of feet on white sand. 'Ahhhh...'

50. 'Who you are' is a sensation; 'what you are' is that which senses

If the belief is present

That this text

Is being read *'by you'*,

Think again.

This text is being read -

And there is 'a sense of you'.

Both are sensed, experienced,

By something beyond…

Invisible, untouchable,

Formless, indestructible

And omnipresent,

This awareness,

This presence,

In which all appears

And disappears

Has been called 'God'

And is *what you are.*

You are 'this' – this awareness going on...

'This' is God:

You are God.

51. There's nothing to fear

There's nothing to fear.

When there's wish-fulfilling

To be something

Or someone -

Nothing *is* fearsome.

But when it's known

There's no one to fear -

Fearlessness

Is everywhere.

52. Absolute contentment is not a possibility: it is reality

One comes to a meeting labelled 'satsang'

Or 'discussions on nonduality'

With the sense that something is missing,

Is to be acquired.

One thinks,

'I am not completely happy,

I need to find happiness -

Or a path to it.

Perhaps I will find that here'.

The truth is

It is solely the belief

That 'something' can 'bring about' 'complete happiness'

That is the cause of unhappiness.

A 'something' (a thing that comes and goes,

May be found and lost - 'a still mind', 'a loving personality')

Is obviously limited, temporary,

And therefore cannot have anything to do with 'completion',

'Absolution'.

As unbelievable as it sounds,

Absolute, perfect contentment

Is already fully manifested in you,

As you.

For this to be seen,

The death of the blinding belief that contentment is elsewhere

Is all that needs to happen.

Any encouragement to meditate or not meditate

Can only reinforce the sense

That contentment is at the end of a process,

Is not already and always the case.

A truly clear seeing knows and expresses

That there is no such thing as 'meditating' and 'not meditating'.

There is only the changeless 'this',

Which is timeless, placeless,

Which wholly exposes as fallacy

All sense that there is anything distinct,

Separate or separable.

So there is no 'process',

No 'meditation', taking place 'here'

And 'not there'.

The exposition of this fallacy

And the clarity that exposes it,

Is the sole occupation

Of nondualistic expression.

On Jesus, Christ, God And The Illusion Of Objectivity

53. 'God the Father' is an object; in reality, there are no objects

One of the most extreme examples of the mind's compulsive propensity to convert 'isness' into 'things' (post ego-formation/pre-ego-dispersion) is evident in the concept 'God', which has come to denote something like the opposite of its original meaning. I say *something like* the opposite', because it is trickier than this. God is everything: nothing is apart or opposed to "Him". But what He has come to represent is effectively the most monumental something or someone imaginable. Perhaps the term 'God the Father' is partly responsible for this. If, as psychotherapists claim, the infant experiences blissful unity with the mother, perhaps 'the father', lurking in the background, distant, appearing and disappearing, represents the first 'object', the first 'external thing', the first sense of separation. The father is the phallus; he is hard and prominent and dominant. He epitomizes what it is to be a something, a somebody. He wants everyone to know that he is there, at the centre, governing. Like 'God the Creator', he is responsible for the creation, the siring and upbringing of the family, and yet his almighty presence represents something autonomous and aloof, the creator separate from his creation, so that, when anything 'bad' or at least unpleasant or displeasing (to him) occurs in the family, it is most certainly 'not his fault'.

This is the popular construct of God – the quintessential Big Daddy. The reality is very different. When awakening happens, when godliness is perceived and embodied, it is seen that there is no one and nothing, that the kind of somebody depicted in popular constructions of the father and The Father represents only a 'not seeing' and denial of pure existential emptiness, and a resultant, reactive effort to be a real somebody – powerful, muscular, phallic; the breadwinner to end all breadwinners. My guess is that the expression usually labelled 'Jesus' or 'Christ' intended 'God the Father' to represent a vanquishing of The Big Daddy, rather than a cosmic-scale reinforcement or reconstruction of it. What awakening reveals is that one is *fathered* not by a male human body, but by consciousness, by 'this', by what is omnipresent, unchanging. All is born out of this: *all* – including, for example, the seeing of a particular form, often a fairly moody, self-important (and also caring and protective) one, labelling itself 'Daddy'. The father Jesus talks of as being God is omnipresent, everywhere and everything, and therefore without form (form being something distinguishable, something somewhere *and not* somewhere else or something else), what he termed 'spirit'. This 'father', then, might be described as the anti-phallus: he is an absolute nobody, a nonentity. In actual fact, God cannot be 'anti' anything: nothingness is as much in the pretending to be a somebody as in the seeing that there is nobody.

The following two poems reflect, in particular ways, these two kinds of fatherhood. The first focuses particularly on the pervasiveness and contagiousness of patriarchy in the psyche, while the latter points to the characterless nature of being by disembodying itself, or rather, by demonstrating that there is no-body.

54. Dramatising the contagiousness of patriarchal objectivisation

Daddy's Boys

Mummy's always in a muddle,
Daddy never is.

Mummy always tries to sing songs
In and out of doors
And tune
And tries to teach us all the words
And always gets them wrong.

Daddy never does.
Daddy isn't like that
And neither are we –
Are we Daddy?

Mummy always cooks things but burns her fingers,
Daddy doesn't.
Mummy always tries to make us laugh but can't,
Daddy doesn't.
Mummy tries to carry things
And always stumbles and fumbles and breaks
Down
And stutters
When she when she
Speaks
And tries to explain
Things
And always is in a muddle.
Daddy never is.
Daddy doesn't like that,
And neither do we –
Do we Daddy?

55. Jesus is thought, which is limited; Christ is boundless oneness

This is Jesus Christ here;
My holiest communication yet;
My appearance apparent here -
Is the lightest bread I can beget.

Can you hear me?
Do you see me?
Smell, taste and touch me.
Five ways to feel this blessed 'somebody'
Shimmering right before thee.

Doubtless I am the presence you sense;
Jesus be the name of these words;
Look - and I vanish like incense:
See this, and as Christ, be Heaven-sent.

56. 'Planet Earth' is myth; there is only Heaven

The propaganda

Is that this is somewhere called 'Planet Earth'

And someone called 'you' lives there.

But have you ever actually encountered this 'Planet Earth'?

You read 'Planet Earth'

And perhaps a sense of a very large or small blue-green orb

Springs to mind,

Or perhaps a mass of different races and species

Lumped together as 'a group'.

But this is just a belief, an image appearing.

Look around.

What actually is the case?

First and foremost,

There is the sense of existence;

There is knowing that something is here, something is going on.

And what is going on,

One sees,

Is the appearance of colours and shapes,

Sounds and smells,

Touches and tastes.

It is *from this only*

That the *secondary* senses

Of 'The World',

'History',

And 'Me and My Life'

Arise.

See that 'space' and 'time'

Are purely concepts arising in a *sense of existence*

That is always present,

Always there,

And changelessly so –

And you will know that there is only eternity,

Only infinity,

Only Heaven.

57. 'Gravity' is a sense generated by the false belief in separation

'Gravity' is the great lie.

It would be better

And more appropriate

If the apple had knocked Newton out cold,

Or stone dead.

(Not really).

What is meant here is that 'gravity' is the whole sleepy illusion.

'Gravity' is the sense that reality is something solid, dense,

Weighty,

And fractured into separate bits called 'objects'

That are pulled and pushed in relation to one another…

The universe a vast mechanical structure

Of moving parts…

Called 'things', 'creatures' and 'people'.

(This 'people'-dream is the one believed with the greatest gravity!)

The truth is,

There is no 'structure',

No 'movement',

And no 'parts'.

There is only consciousness,

Which is not located anywhere,

Is indivisibly present

And timelessly so.

When it is known that there is nothing solid,

And nothing separate -

All there is

Is light.

Love Loves

58. Commendation creates condemnation: love lies beyond valuation

A Christian friend of mine is constantly 'amazed', or at least he uses the word 'amazing' very regularly. He means it as compliment, and so the activity is what society might regard as a very positive, affirmative, embracing thing. It is not at all though. If certain happenings are certified as 'amazing', other happenings are, by implication, considered less valuable. And the more compliments are dished out, the more inferior seems the 'not amazing' minority. The activity represents a very subtle, insidious power, then; in one stroke it can condemn and marginalize (through omission), yet at the same time the apparent person administering this treatment (a gushing affirmation here, a hyperbolic declaration there) is thought of as a very 'affirmative', 'accepting', 'complementary' individual, a real saint. Where no valuation, no comparison, neither commendation nor condemnation, are – here lies acceptance, love and freedom. It is everywhere; it accepts everything, *including* rejection and the kind of selective, marginalizing 'acceptance' discussed above. This is goodness. This is Godliness: the absolute love God is.

59. Oneness is all-embracing

It is gracefulness
And unspeakably disgraceful;
Indiscriminate,
And the racist himself.

It is everything;
It is all-embracing -
The love of hate,
The hate of love:

So graceful it floats everywhere -
Disgracefully into your underwear!

60. Love loves

Love loves the papist,
The faithless,
The sacrilegious;
Love loves the honest,
The true-faced,
The two-faced;
Love loves the brave-faced,
The face-paint,
The needlepoint;
Love loves the wayward,
The racist,
The rapist.

61. 'Oneness' and 'sex' are unrelated

Nondualistic perception and sex have been the major subjects of this text. Other texts also have these two themes as their principal topics. Many of these other texts are, however, involved in forging connections between sexuality and 'spirituality'. For example, they say things like 'Celibacy facilitates a build up of energy that may be sufficient to ignite enlightenment' or 'Having lots of sex makes a person very open and sensual and therefore ready to embrace the nondual perspective' or 'Once awakening happens, the sex-drive disappears since there is no longer any polarity, no longer the sense that I am over here and I want to get my mitts on that, mysterious, almost unattainable beauty over there'. This is utter bollocks. This text here knows and expresses that the nondual is sexual, asexual, celibate, pre-sexual, menopausal, inanimate – everything and nothing. The nondual has nothing to do with any specifics - behavioural, sexual or otherwise. It is pure omnipresence. This text here only addresses both 'the sexual' and 'the nondual' because both are energizing, productive subjects for this writing organism, and because the former provides comic, energetic interludes for entertainment and relief purposes! Rather than suggest that there is any special link between sexuality and awakening, this text explains and demonstrates that nonduality is absolutely everywhere, everything, including that, 'sex', which has been daftly valued as the basest, lowest of things (for example, in mainstream Christianity) and elsewhere as a particularly 'high', 'sacred' something (in Tantra, for instance). Also, the periodic appearance of the sexual in this text reflects the normal periodic arising of sexual desire in this body sitting here, watching these little black squiggles appear. If this weren't the case, though, if a total absence of sex-drive, or on the contrary, a permanent state of arousal was present, that would be totally fine, just 'what is'. Peel off the judgement, the valuation, and a blissful intelligence that is simplicity is revealed.

62. Oneness is fearlessness that may manifest as fear

There is no question that awakening brings with it a certain sense of security, of invincibility, of fearlessness. Last night, at our housewarming party, it didn't matter one bit that this body-mind wasn't entering into any conversations for quite a while. There weren't the accompanying senses of being looked down upon, being left behind, being thought of as boring, empty. There were just tensions disappearing in relaxation and, as it happened, alcoholic intoxication, and then at some point conversation began and continued. Both bits were calm, assured and satisfying.

As an appendage to this, it must be emphasised that feelings such as 'alienation', 'isolation', and 'misery' can happen within the awakened perception. At a different party, very recently (several months after the event just described above), an emotional and behavioural tendency of this organism caused a sense of exclusion from proceedings to happen, and frustration and tears subsequently. The body craves affection, emotions crave intimacy, thinking craves interaction…whether it is believed that this has something to do with 'persons' or whether is known to be actually the play of consciousness – it makes no difference.

In a way, awakening will almost certainly bring about a specific instance of social isolation. There is the seeing of a magical, exhilarating secret – that is very rarely received.

63. There is nothing but awareness

Is the belief present that 'you' are 'over there',

Reading 'this notice' that is 'over here'?

'In what' or rather '*to* what' does this believing,

This sense of 'space',

And this sense of a 'you', happen?

It happens to awareness.

You are the awareness in which a sense of a 'you' has manifested,

But this 'you' is nothing but awareness.

Awareness is impersonal and characterless.

What you are is infinitude, which is nothing.

Enlightenment Has Nothing To Do With Suffering

64. Nonduality has nothing to do with suffering

Having just watched that motion picture entitled *Gandhi*, the thought arises that those various verbal expressions that coincide, without fail, with the lip-movement of that tiny body labelled 'Gandhi' are highly intelligent instructions for the diminishing of suffering. This is what all politics, law, doctoring and psychotherapy is, or should be, concerned with – the minimization of suffering, unhappiness. This expression has nothing to do with that. (If there was a particular verbal expression that happened to coincide with the lip-movement of a body labelled 'Siddartha Gautama' or 'Buddha' that once said 'Liberation is the end of all suffering', it was having an off-day). What this expression, nondualism, is concerned with is that which is in both suffering and pleasure in equal and infinite measure: that which is both pleasure and suffering at once. That which never succeeds or fails, or ever moves anywhere.

This expression does not contradict or criticize the activity of minimizing the potentiality of suffering. Pain arises and the body takes a paracetamol. (Or doesn't.) Being forced to travel third-class on the ground of skin-colour, or some fiction known as 'race', happens and then follows a little bald-headed voice preaching 'non-violence' and 'Indian rule'. It is a natural process.

Sometimes this tackling of suffering is confused with the message occurring here, in these lines. Somehow the idea comes about that nonduality has something to do with 'peace', 'harmony' and 'happiness'. The difference between the two is very easy to spot. With that expression labelled 'Mahatma Gandhi' one sees advocateship, the recommendation of a certain doing over another doing; for example, 'Non-violence is more likely to bring about Indian-rule than violence', 'People are more productive and happier if they are in competition with their fellow men than if they work together' and 'Meditation is better for you than heroine'. With *this* expression, here now, one observes a tripping over oneself in order to avoid any recommendation whatsoever. The first is concerned with change, with a positive shift in the pleasure/suffering ratio; the second expresses the seeing that that which apparently changes is actually dead still, changeless, and always immaculate, whether hell, non-violent purgation, or utopia be the happening.

65. Sticks and stones may break bones, but···

Sticks and stones may break bones,
But insults *always* hurt 'me'.
For all my fame is but a name,
And I obscene in obscenity.

Just to explain, there is no 'name',
Just a feeling called 'continuity',
For a certain pain and the sound 'name' -
All discontinuous, dismembering 'me'.

So sticks and stones may break bones
But they can never hurt 'me'.
For I am but a dreamy ghost,
No stone's throw – from being free.

66. Absolute contentment is unattainable

Absolute contentment is unattainable.

That which is reached
Is temporary.

That which comes
Goes.

The Absolute,
On the other hand,
Is always the case,
Is unavoidable.

And being so,
It accepts everything,
It *is* everything,
It is discontented with nothing.

A contentment
That is content
With discontent

Is impregnable,
Absolute.

This is the presence
That is never absent.

67. The elimination of suffering is not equal to absolute happiness

Suffering and the treatment of it are hugely complex issues. As such, it is all too easy to think simplistically in this area. For instance, the reading of this book takes place, and thought reacts as follows:

> What good is this? What value has 'knowing I am formless awareness' when there is such widespread and intense suffering in the world? If the energy spent propagating nondualism was put instead into feeding and healing suffering bodies, *that* would be valuable, *that* would be helpful, *that* would bring greater happiness into the world.

Such linear thinking simply won't do here. For example, consider the fact that suicide rates are vastly greater in affluent regions than in poverty-stricken areas. While a malnourished, disease-ridden African is struggling with whatever energy he can summon to live but one more day, a wealthy, healthy European businessman is preparing to end his life. Where lies the greater suffering? How can suffering be measured?

I don't pretend to have answers to these questions. To me, the pertinent, concrete point in this is the fact that a universally well-nourished, healthy, affluent global population is not the same as a universally happy society (the suicide consideration above might even suggest the opposite).

What about happiness then? How can that be brought about? If happiness lies in pleasure, then that happiness is on extremely shaky ground; in the ending of that pleasure, or the onset of pain, it is gone.

Perhaps it is believed that happiness cannot be a permanent fixture.

It can be. If this is not the case in your experience, this is purely because you haven't experienced it yet! What nondualistic expression seeks to communicate is the fact that perception is perception, regardless of the nature of it. Whatever appears, appears in a consciousness, a presence, a 'this', that is always and only the case. As such, it does not come and go; and therefore, it does not lie in any temporal appearances, such as 'suffering' and 'pleasure' (or, one might say, it lies in *all* temporal experiences). Of course, depending on one's use of words, one might say 'Happiness is temporary; it vanishes, for example, in sadness'. The 'happiness' this text has been referring to in this passage, however, lies in the senses of freedom, fulfilment, peacefulness, homeliness, intimacy and fearlessness that come from knowing the formlessness, completeness, unicity and infinity of that which you are, that which is, 'what is'.

This text is not saying that a decrease in suffering is not a desirable, valuable occurrence. It *is* desirable: there is the desire for pleasure and the absence of pain (except when pain is pleasurable). What this text *is* saying is that suffering is not absolutely eliminable; the elimination of it is not equal to happiness; and that a complete, permanent happiness, one that lies in sadness and in all things, is a reality, and in fact, is the only reality. And this reality may be indicated by expressions such as this text: so (Mr Imaginary Challenger above!), this textual energy is not wasted, misplaced.

This passage is incomplete on the subject of suffering; it is very far from being watertight. But this is the case with all verbalisation: it is something limited, formal, tiny, endlessly incomplete. Luckily, this is not a philosophical treatise; it doesn't matter if it does a bad job of pretending to 'cover everything'. All that is relevant here, and what is really taking place, is a gesturing towards something that is so familiar, unavoidable, it is missed. It is not so much a case of 'not seeing the forest for the trees' but rather 'not seeing the seeing for the seeing'. That is to say, since there is never any 'not seeing' to compare the seeing with, to define the seeing by, since there is only seeing, seeing goes unnoticed (until it doesn't, until it *is* noticed).

(Incidentally, if one takes 'the forest' as 'consciousness', 'sensing', and 'the trees' as 'the content of consciousness', 'sensation' – 'not seeing the forest for the trees' becomes an applicable saying. For visual sensation in particular, 'forest' is especially apposite: the infinite varieties of form and colour can seem like a bewildering jungle of information, in which one becomes lost, confused, hypnotised into the hallucinatory sense of separation.)

There Is Only Supple Consciousness

68. There is only supple consciousness

Some text is called 'coverage'.

Journalism 'covers' the event.

Something happens

And then a body with a microphone

Or laptop computer

Outputs a mass of words…

But these words have nothing to do with the event –

How can they?

The event is the event,

Words are words.

Such text is a 'cover-up';

It covers up that which it pretends to describe.

To disintegrate matters further

The fact is,

There isn't anything that can be called 'an event'.

There is nothing that is singular, solid,

Distinguishable, autonomous,

Actual.

Reading this,

Here, now,

Is not 'an event'.

There are colours,

White and black *here*,

And millions more

Reds and blues

In a million hues;

There's a sense of perspective,

This page 'here', that body 'there' ;

Shapes –

These rectangles and squiggles.

But where is 'the event'?

Where is there anything set in cement?

There is only supple consciousness;

This is only supple consciousness,

Appearing and disappearing...

As everything.

69. This is nothing but timeless omnipresence

Nondualistic expression seeks to reveal that which is timeless, that which is always present, that which is everywhere, whilst at the same time showing that that which appears to come and go, live and die, and that which seems to be somewhere and not somewhere else…that all of this is nothing but the timelessness, the omnipresence.

70. This is indefinable; it is a 'this' that is 'not this'

Philosophy is defined as....

So this is not philosophy.

This is indefinable.

Neither is this 'nonduality'.

'Nonduality' is a word and therefore a definition;

This is indefinable.

A thoughtful definition and label for this

Is Jiddu Krishnamurti's expression

'This whatever-it-is'.

Only,

It is neither an 'it'

Nor an 'is',

And to call it an 'it and not it' or 'is and isn't'

(Which is better)

Is to convey the sense of an untrue division

Between 'it' and 'not it', 'is' and 'isn't'

When *this*, that which is happening here,

The nature of nature,

Is seen as an 'it' *that is* a 'not it';

An 'is' *that is* an 'isn't' –

Then that's it!

71. Twilight aches of reality revealing itself, or not

This time of day, this time of night, twilight, has always seemed to me to be drenched in oneness revealing itself. It aches of this. Colours and shapes and the boundaries between them melt into the deepening darkness. Of course, it must always be restated that there is only oneness revealing itself, that this cannot increase or decrease in quantity or intensity, it is always absolute, and that if for any apparent person twilight does not ache of oneness revealing itself, this means nothing. This 'not experiencing' is oneness revealing itself as 'not experiencing'. Still, it's fun to be poetic about it!

72. The only fact there is, is called 'being' and 'life'

The only fact there is

Is called 'being' and 'life'.

Some say,

'Humans are the only beings.'

Others say,

'All plants and animals are living things,

But plastic and rocks

Are not.'

Forget this confusion,

This complexity.

There is no such thing as 'that' or 'me'.

There are no 'lives', no 'beings' –

Just life, which is being,

Which is 'this',

Right here,

Right now.

Always

And in all ways...

Being is all:

Teething

Cliff-erosion

Weeping

Sheet-raining

This book

Is alive

As the hands holding it -

Look how I speak

And gesture

And live;

And there's the rock

That some say 'is not',

But see how it *is*:

See how it lives...

(Without feeling, or breath, It *is*,
Nevertheless.)

There Is No 'Other'

73. Dissatisfaction comes from belief in otherness

This – what is the case now and at any time – only appears to be inadequate, less than immaculate, when the belief arises that 'something else', 'somewhere else' or 'someone else' would be better. Lounging on the bed with a hangover, it would be better if I were outdoors in the sun, 'making the most of the day', or finally getting round to filling in those taxation forms, or not alone, out at the beach with my friends, or if I could muster the energy to finally write an impressive, admirable novel, or if I were an effortlessly great movie star, living in luxury. Notice that these kinds of fantasies tend to generate dissatisfaction with what is actually the case and not vice versa; it is not that dissatisfaction with what is actually the case generates these kinds of fantasies. When it is seen that wherever you apparently go, however glamorous, however mundane, *this*, this awareness, this beingness, and only this, is what is present, it is known that things could not be any different from how they already are. And how they are is meticulous, exquisite. Feeling rundown, having a cold, in boredom, listlessness, and loneliness – see that it is only the belief in the possibility of something other than 'what is' that generates misery. Without that you will find that a sense of completion, rightness, satisfaction is felt, whatever the case.

74. 'Self' is a certain sense, sensed by selflessness

This sense of 'yourself'

Is that of a sort of 'shadowy structure',

Imagined to be lurking somewhere

Behind a pair of eyes.

See it as this

Or any other way

And see that you are not that fearful, imprisoning agglomeration.

You are the seer,

That which sees

Everything that is seen.

And that which sees

Is forever hidden from sight,

Eternally safe.

Being invisible,

You are infinite and immortal,

Formless and so invincible.

75. I am as much this book, as I am this body (an email)

Hi Stephen,

I'll be up front about this and say immediately that I want to tell you more about the kind of thing I have written to you about in the past - to do with perceiving. I say this because whenever I talk about it, there is an anxiety that the listener may think I am trying to force something down his throat... that it is a sort of Jehovah's Witness thing. I hope it's clear that it's not like that at all - I have no wish for anybody to believe in anything or to agree with me on anything. I just have a bursting desire to talk about my experience, simply because it is like a secret that I keep being reminded of, all the time, but that I generally can't talk about, because it doesn't easily slot into normal conversation. I'll stop explaining myself to death and hope that what I say shows that I have no intentions...other than simply the enjoyment of communicating something that fascinates me.

I remember when I wrote to you last about this, I talked in terms of an experience that could come and go, that happened 'to me' and that was something 'heavenly'. I also talked about 'enlightened masters'. It actually slightly makes me squirm to recall this kind of talk now, because it has become clear that it is wholly misguided... and I really don't like taste of it!

What has happened since then is impossible to explain. Language is a big problem with this sort of thing. The closest I can get to explaining it is to say that before the end of April I perceived things in terms of me being someone called Guy walking around in a world that was 'out there'. I was 'here'... (behind this nose perhaps) and the universe was 'out there'... I was sitting 'here', at the computer, and the computer screen was 'over there'. And then, after April, the perception was very different. This nose, this body, that computer screen, the hills out of the window and what had previously been experienced as a separate, objective, external reality – all this was suddenly experienced as one indivisible thing, happening in what I am. You see the language problems? It sounds absurd! Another way of putting it is that, by-and-large, there is no identifying with any particular arising in consciousness: pain happens, thinking happens, the sound of a car driving past happens, a chair happens - and there is no object-subject differentiation made between these, no sense that 'that is me' and 'that is not me'.

Funnily enough, identification still can happen - the mind can start getting all involved with 'what people think of me', 'how can I become amazing and be liked and respected by everyone' - but the tendency now is that this happens, it is then noticed that it is just another thing arising in what I am (aka 'awareness' or 'thisness')... and then it tends to peter out fairly rapidly.

Does it make any sense? In these first few months (and I have often read that this is very common early on) it has sometimes seemed very off-balancing and peculiar. On the one hand, there is this seeing of an 'I am-ness' that is totally beyond the arising of 'body', 'mind', 'life' and so forth - that is still, timeless, unlocated; and in this, then, I see that there isn't really any 'time' or 'space' or 'life', because all these appearances are really made out of a consciousness or 'thisness' that is formless, that is nothing. Does that make sense? Sometimes the analogy of a cinema screen is used: it looks as though there are lots of separate things - some called objects, some called subjects - moving about in time and space; but actually there is just a flat, undivided screen that is dead still. So you could say 'The infinite appears as the finite', but I think that just ends up sounding very grand and conceptual, and it doesn't communicate the 'taste' of it at all. So yes, this keeps being seen again and again - and yet within the appearance, there is still this body that needs feeding, this mind that wants entertaining... so it can feel a strange realisation, almost like 'a predicament' (though it isn't).

76. 'Look for the dead bodies within' (a dream and response to it)

A few weeks back,

The following dream occurred.

A figure

I once called 'my father'

Appeared and spoke about 'choice' and 'responsibility'.

The figure

I once called 'myself'

Then replied with the proposition

That there is no volition:

Only spontaneous occurrence.

'My father' then said,

'It's like when St John of the Cross says,

'Look for the dead bodies within'.

Look for the dead bodies within.

I awoke to the feeling that 'my father' had agreed with 'me'.

He was saying,

'That which is called "me" or 'free-will'

Is actually dead,

Is a phantom'.

'Me' *is* a delusional thought only.

Last night,

A second understanding came.

Yesterday,

A dry, rubbery, gripping contraction

Was 'here' - suspended in consciousness.

It was like a foreign-body or a corpse –

Floating here.

This was 'a dead body within'.

I thought, last night,

Perhaps my father's statement

Actually supported his belief in volition.

He was saying,

That that dead body, that body of past feeling,

Provokes certain reactions,

Determines behaviours and occurrences,

And is therefore a sort of 'power' or 'will'.

Regardless,

What is clear

Is that the statement is directing attention to this 'thing'.

I believe,

Though I could be wrong,

That the absolute decay or cremation of this corpse,

Where nothing remains,

But supple sensation,

Is equal to the final adjustment,

To the final realisation

(That 'happened' here now six months ago).

The realisation

That there is only awareness -

Awareness without character

Or form.

77. My laughable beliefs about enlightenment

There is no greater comic than the mind. The beliefs it dreams up are hilarious. Just to narrow it down a bit, may I share with you some of the funny things this brain here believed about enlightenment, prior to its actual emergence? I believed I would suddenly be surrounded by a mighty golden-glowing force-field of energy that at various times would be noticed by particularly perceptive people, who would then, if male, prostrate themselves at my feet and beg to follow me to the ends of The Universe, and if female, would rip their clothes off, hurl themselves at me, or simply swoon at the sheer majesty of me… Well – something like this!!

I believed that I would be incapable of making an error. Funnily enough, when I teasingly told my Hindu girlfriend that 'I am enlightened' she immediately told me I couldn't be – because I have eczema! This is very much the same mindset. In a way, though, I was right. Error is impossible; 'what is' is only ever immaculate. But this does not mean always getting from A to B without taking a wrong turning or never spilling one's fifth pint: it means that these actions, these things we have labelled 'errors', are seen to be perfect, fine, funny and beautiful…impossible to better.

I believed that I would never be fearful of anything. The truth is, if this body is walking down a street and nearing a cluster of aggressive-looking teenagers, it gets nervous. Bodies don't like to be hurt – whether they know there is nobody and nothing or not!

I believed I would suddenly be irresistibly attractive, magnetic. I honestly believed that my eyes would suddenly be far more shiny…as if lit up from inside. I believed I would move with grace and total confidence like the elf in *Lord of the Rings* or John Wayne or something. And I believed that I would become the most fantastic lover imaginable – effortlessly lasting forever, women orgasming left, right and centre. Of course, these things may *very well* be true. But that would just happen to be lucky coincidence. Ahem.

Anyhow, the point is, awakening has nothing to do with behaviour, capability, state of mind or any aspect of the appearance. What is seen is that everything, no matter how average or hopeless, selfish or ugly the conditioned mind judges it to be, is perfect, is perfection itself. There is only oneness, and as such no one is responsible, no one is in charge. Volition implies something separate, something that can stand aside. There is no such thing.

As an appendage, it is pertinent to note that my beliefs about enlightenment were basically synonymous with my desires for enlightenment and my desires generally. And, as you can see, these basically boil down to pure sex-drive, libido. For any species that has survived aeons of the cutthroat natural selection to prosper presently, a fierce reproductive impulse is inevitable. Because of the unflattering (to the ego-snob) neanderthal simplicity of this fact, the mind loves to interpret, translate and obscure it into a zillion and one rationalisations such as 'I make love in order that kundalini shoots up my spine and I become divine', or 'I like talking to members of the opposite sex because they have such an interesting perspective on things', or 'It's good, healthy exercise – that's all', or 'I only spend hours gawping at the Sistine Chapel ceilings for purely artistic, aesthetic purposes', or 'yes predominantly female congregations flock to see powerful preaching men in black cassocks, but so what?', or 'No one told me *that* was sex; my doctor told me it was merely a breathing exercise?'. Sometimes ruthless honesty, however crude and gratuitous, especially when crude and gratuitous, is a nice relief from the efforts of denial, affirmation and excuse.

78. Reality is fiction

This, this text here, and also this life happening right now, this reading, *is* a David Lynch movie. In 'a David Lynch movie' one finds a world, or worlds, periodically dissolving into what is both 'consciousness' and 'energy'. In *Lost Highway*, two characters temporarily (and infinitely) evaporate in the energetic bliss of orgasm, which is also a blinding white flash of lightning in the skies. In *Twin Peaks: Fire Walk With Me* one sees electric-power pylons making 'wooing' sounds, and then black-and-white television interference dissolving the waking world into a dreamland, in which a midget stands on a floor of jagged black-and-white stripes and pronounces 'I sound like this…woo woo woo…' For Lynch, energy and consciousness, matter and mind are one. There is no energy and no consciousness – there is only 'this'.

Here, in this text, *I* am the midget 'wooing'. I, your narrator, am so small I do not exist: this is but ink. And yet I go 'woo woo woo'; there is sound happening, this is energy sounding, energy appearing as words. In a way, it would be better if me, this sounding, were simply to say 'woo' or 'rhubarb rhubarb'. Semantics, words concerned with meaning, are that which activates the time-machine, that which conveys the sense of something important to be discovered or learnt somewhere else, on the next page, in two chapters' time, at the end of this sentence. But there is nothing else, nothing but this - no deep and mysterious understanding to ascertain. There is just woo woo woo woo…

Most commonly, a movie's power, its capacity to move, lies in its believability, its successfulness in generating what is called 'disavowal', in helping the viewer to convince himself that what is appearing on screen is 'true', while knowing that it isn't. Lynch movies turn this on its head. Instead they expose the fictionality of that which has been labelled 'reality'; they point to the fact that there is nothing substantial, objective: examine anything and it disintegrates into empty consciousness. As such, these movies have unprecedented power: where other movies rely on the incomplete force of disavowal, the pretending not to know that one knows that this movie is fictional, Lynch movies tear down the veiled separation of 'real' and 'fictional', pouring themselves out of the screen and into the living room…showing that *this*, this life, this appearance of a body sat in front of a film screen or book, is no more real than a movie. This *is* a movie, purely an appearance of movement, of colours, sounds, and characters, made of total stillness, emptiness, nothing.

As the apparently separate images appearing on the screen, the different characters, warring and making love, the unfolding plot, the thickening subplot, the sickening dialogue – as all of this is nothing but light, so are we, so is this, pure awareness.

79. 'Spiritual tradition' promotes a sense of separation (a dream)

Last night, I gave my third 'satsang'. My first basically involved my friend Phil asking me questions while visiting me on holiday. The second is this current, ongoing process of talking to my computer. This third instance, last night, took place in the fair realm of dreamland. A group of around 20 to 30 hippies gathered in 'The Meditation Room' of 'The Relaxation Centre', located near Pembroke Road in Bristol. I was informed that the discussion would be preceded by one particular hippy playing some music, some woodwind Asian instrument I for some dreamy reason supposed. But there was no music, only a collective chanting of the word 'ohm' that is a nasal, flat, droning sound. I then spent the next 15 minutes before waking up vigorously explaining that chanting the word 'ohm' is not a good idea, because it is associated with something called 'a tradition' and, what's more, a tradition that is supposedly in some way connected with awakening. But, I said, I do not recommend that you don't chant the word 'ohm' either because then the mind just thinks, 'Ah! that's the way; this is how to become "good", "clear" or "conscious" enough for enlightenment'. The association of awakening with 'Asia', 'all things Asian', is a very daft idea. Awakening is the seeing that there is no such thing as 'Asia', no such thing as 'tradition' and no such thing as 'awakening'. Maintaining any sense of tradition, of history and of ceremony and path, can only serve to solidify a sense that there is some big, material structure, called something like 'time and space'. It makes the story so much more convincing, so much denser and more agglomerate, which is fine and full of fun, but which represents, at the same time, the continuing of hypnotism, the perpetuation of the sense that there is a material world of individuals, societies, nations and so forth. This is the dream. There is just 'this'. Not even 'the book' you think is here in your hands. Just 'this'...colours, forms...all fluid, disconnected, infinitesimally transient...nothing there - nothing 'real', 'solid', 'objective'. Nothing like 'a book', 'hands', or even 'colour'; let alone 'history' or 'tradition'.

Unity Has Nothing
To Do With
Unicity

80. Oneness is the whole gamut

Leaves

When our eyes meet,
Heat-up and melt,
In searing love weld -
A great wind shakes through this body,
Raking away dead leaves of memory,
Dead leaves of many,
Dead leaves of body,
And finally,
When nothing is left,
Nothing sounds this song.
And when it is sung,
The silent space
Is the winter sun…
Stinging with little lights,
For fun,
And throbbing with such subtleties.
This is permanence,
Permeation,
Presence, essence,
Emanation;
It's in everything,
It *is* everything…
The singer is drowned in her own singing,
No blame, choice, or chance in this sounding,
Of winning,
Or sinning,
Or of anything.
And all that is left,
After all has left,
The leaves, the wind, the song, its breath
(And while it is all still here as well),
All that is -
Is this.

81. Unity has nothing to do with unicity

That which is called 'unity' and that which is called 'unicity' are absolutely unrelated. 'Unicity' is oneness that is indivisible and limitless. 'Unity' is a wholeness that is both divisible and limited. It is a thing, a unit, formed of smaller units uniting together. 'Unity' is synonymous with words like 'wholeness', 'integration', 'harmony' and 'grouping'. Perhaps the easiest way to comprehend the absolute differences between 'unicity' and 'unity' is to think in terms of space and nothingness. A unit is a thing. For example, the human body is a unity of flesh, blood, bones and so forth, or of legs, arms, torso, or of systems, respiratory, reproductive, etc, or of organs, of cells, or atoms. The unity can be measured; it is here, above the toes and from the head downwards, and not there, where, say, a different body, or a radiator is. It is a definite form and holds a definite place in space. Even a 'comm-unity', supposedly composed of immeasurable units called 'humans', is here – where lips proclaim 'I am a sannyasin', and not there, where the words 'I am not a sannyasin' or 'I eat Big Macs' happen.

'Unicity', on the other hand, might be thought of in terms of 'nothingness'. You are just about to go to bed and the room in which you sit is illuminated by a bedside lamp. What is seen is divisible, made up of unity - there is a bed, furniture, a lamp, a body and so on. Switch out the light and all that is gone. All units, all objects, all demarcation and division has vanished. There is not even a room left – no walls, floor or ceiling. The 'blackness' or 'nothingness' is without limit, and indivisible. This is a reasonable analogy as to what unicity is. However, it is decidedly imperfect, the reasons for which will become apparent shortly.

The reason this difference between 'unity' and 'unicity' is being cited here is that many so-called nondualistic expressions erroneously speak as if these two were the same thing, or at least related. For example, the communication may be that living harmoniously, without conflict, has some relevance to enlightenment, to unicity. Or perhaps, that living in a particular community, with what are called 'a master' and 'fellow disciples', has something to do with it. Both cases are highly compelling. In the latter, for example, something that is often called 'communion' can come about, and which is more likely to come about here than in other settings. 'Communion' is where a unit is formed - say, by lots of bodies sitting silently together with closed eyes, or, by 'the master' and 'a disciple' making eye-contact - and as a result a certain 'energy' is felt; an energy that seems to dissolve the room, to lie before the room, that feels both ancient and perfectly fresh, that is timeless and, like the 'blackness' of the analogy above, placeless, limitless.

So, it seems that a specific arrangement, a certain form of unit or unity, can bring about an emergence of unicity. This is the fallacy. Backed up by the emotional intensity of the emergent experience it is the most convincing and therefore hindering fallacy one can come across. First and foremost, unicity is not that experience of energy. Unicity is absolutely unavoidable, it is right here in the feeling of separateness, it is the mundanity of reading a book. It is in confusion and the mistaken belief that this isn't it: it *is* that belief! And yes, it is in blissful energetic states, *but no more so than at any other moment*. The simultaneous sensation of ancientness and freshness in such special experiences convinces one that this is the timeless, this is the omnipresent, the absolute, and yet one moment it is there and the next moment comes the sense of separateness and frustration. What kind of absolute is here one minute and gone the next? The absolute, unicity, is unavoidable and always the case. Energetic sensations come and go; they are but limited units of the appearance.

The transcendental state is the most powerful mechanism for keeping the illusion of separateness alive, since the sensual impact of it is so impressive. It happens, and the belief occurs, 'This is unicity!' It is not. The experience vanishes and, because the arrangement was so specific, so formal, so idiosyncratic, the belief arises, 'It must have had something to do with that peculiar setting I was in, with "the master", or "the ashram", with my eyes being shut, with the silence of everybody, or the prolonged eye-contact with the important looking fellow on the pedestal'. Unicity has nothing to do with these specifics. It is everything; it is unavoidable. You are that right now – you have always been, and you have never missed it. There is no need to look for what is already seen.

82. The seeing of oneness can manifest as a sense of dislocation

When it is seen that all there is is sensation (no objects, no mind, no thoughts), perception burns with colour, vigour and splendour. The golden burning can be so intense, so fiery, that it melts the boundaries of everything. It is psychedelic, it is a Picasso painting of a warped face, or warped faces...where no face is left...just floating debris. One aspect of the inappropriateness of the word 'unity' for describing oneness is that the word gives the sense of units being stuck together with a sort of centripetal pull. In actuality, it feels, if anything, like the opposite of this - like a collapsing, or an explosion. It can appear like suddenly everything is disassociated and unravelling - simply floating, present.

This may sound contrary to the mind's concept of what unicity should be like, but remember, oneness is not where all things appear the same, but the knowing that one *is* everything in all its multifarious splendour. Impossibly, in terms of logic at least, the awakened perspective reveals both a more intense awareness of the differentiation and uniqueness of all that manifests, and at the same time the seeing that all this is of the same substance, or the same non-substance, the same insubstantiality.

Even talking in terms of 'seeing nothing' is misleading, and is in a sense imprisoning. There is no seeing - seeing is made out of nothing, there is just nothing. Then there is just collapsing, relaxing, dissolving, freedom. It is like absolutely everything there is breathing as one, or a breeze through all of this, a freshness. The white gleam of sunlight upon water, so bright that everything else is blinded out, everything burns 'til even that gleam is gone. One describes this one way, for example, in terms of burning and melting, and immediately and directly one is aware that it is in fact also exactly the opposite of this. For example, every bit as much as it can seem like a burning and melting of things, it can seem like a cooling, darkening, dispersing... a vast black-hole sitting behind everything that is seen, and the sense of being sucked into it, expanding and disappearing as it. Talk about it in any way, using any words, any terms, and this is misguiding because saying 'It is these words' implies that it is not other words; and yet it is everything, so really it is indescribable... and yet 'un-indescribable'...it cannot *not* be described!

83. Agenda promotes a sense of separation that induces destruction

I have just listened to a tape in which a so-called teacher declares the need to 'wake up' in order that the natural world be protected - polar bears, great white sharks, icecaps.

It sounds like a noble sentiment, but the reality here is that the gun pointed at the polar bear is just re-aimed at the foot of him who may be capable of stopping the destruction.

This is how it is.

The teaching above is the very kind of hallucinogenic narcotic that postpones the awakening it advocates and, if its logic is correct, perpetuates destruction through sleepy greed.

Sleepiness is the belief that there is a big wide world 'out there' - Antarctica, tropical rain forests, the stars, the street outside your house.

The above teaching confirms this belief.

The reality, and the uncompromising, relentless expression of true nonduality, is that *there is nothing*.

Don't imagine or conceptualise this. This is neither 'negative' nor 'denialistic'. Look anywhere and you will see that nothing is solid, static, separate…it all melts into emptiness, pure awareness.

Now, if this and *only this* is expressed and received, felt, known, it may happen that greed will lessen, and destruction with it. The hypothesis goes that since awakening exposes the fallacy that there is anything other than changeless timelessness, the compulsion of repetition (intoning beliefs, comfort eating, describing the same life-story over and over), the fearful need to create the sense of a continuous self, a life, drops away and desire with it.

This may be so, to some degree, but if the reality of nothingness is not expressed without compromise, sleepiness continues, and the teacher keeps his job.

84. Reality consists of nothingness appearing as something

While 'unity' is something that should not be confused with 'unicity', the term does have its uses in this particular expression going on here. For a purpose that shall be revealed shortly, let a hyphen be placed in 'unit' to make 'un-it'. The unit is the appearance of the thing, the object, the 'it'. It is that which appears, that divisible appearance called variously 'life', 'the world', 'space and time', 'existence'. But what is seen in awakening is that all of this appearance apparently going on is made and born of nothing. It is not hard and deep and structured as we imagine it to be: examine any aspect of it and it vanishes in thin air. There is no such thing as 'a thing'; there is just empty consciousness, thisness. So suddenly all 'its' are seen to be 'un-its' – 'its', things, that are at once nothing. Paradoxically, 'it-ness', 'is-ness', is a metaphor for nothingness, 'isn't-ness'. The appearance of form is the invitation to see that here is just formlessness: all 'its' are unmaking themselves, 'un-ing' themselves; they are 'un-its'. In the light of this formulation, it is comical and apt to note that perhaps the greatest, most populated, and powerful societal 'unit' in existence is called 'The UN'. It is one great big nothing!

85. There is no such thing as 'abstract' or 'abstraction'

There is no such thing as 'abstract' or 'abstraction'.

There is only 'this' – which is indivisible.

That which is believed to be 'abstract' is called 'thought'.

(Neither is there any such thing as 'thought').

'Thought' consists of aural, visual and tangible happenings

That are imagined to be 'one thing'.

This imaginary sense of unity is itself a sensory happening,

'A feeling',

Which, like the other happenings (visual, aural and tangible),

Is actually wholly unrelated to all other manifestations.

There is no 'unity' and there is no 'relations' -

All there is is oneness.

The sense of 'abstraction' is synonymous with the sense of 'unity'.

For example, there is the black squiggly visual formation 'red',

The visual appearance of the colour red,

The aural arising of the sound 'red' or 'read',

And perhaps the feeling-manifestation of 'energy', 'passion',

'violence' or 'fieriness'.

All of these distinct, unrelated appearances

Are imagined as one unified thing, called 'a thought'.

Imagined to be consisting of a special relationship

(That is specifically between the above sensate occurrences, and not others)

This imaginary 'unity' or 'unit' also appears to be 'abstract',

'Separate', 'individual'.

It is the same with those imaginary somethings known as

'Objects'

(Rather, 'thought' is 'an object').

For example, it is imagined that there is such a thing as 'a chair'.

Actually, all there is, is certain colours and shapes,

Perhaps the feeling of softness and relaxation

And the appearance of the sound 'ahhhhhh...'

There is no 'chair' somehow 'amongst', 'inside',

'Encompassing' or 'beyond'

These disassociated happenings.

It is the same with all 'things':

'America', 'Planet Earth', 'river', 'life', 'person',

'The Battle of Waterloo'...

There are none of these things,

There is no such thing as anything:

'Things' are myth.

Reality Is Holey-
ness;
All There Is,
Is Dislocation

86. 'Not labelling' is a radically transformed perception

The conditioned mind cannot believe what a radically transformative experiential, existential impact the activity of 'labelling' has. This morning, my awakening to the day was like this. My dreaming involved being in the midst of some highly vigorous, potent, engulfing drama, that must in some way have comprised echoes of one or more movies I have watched. I say this because at some point in my gradual waking-up, the thoughts 'Oh, this is a movie' followed later by 'OH, this is a dream!' appeared. The effect of these thoughts was cataclysmic. One moment, here was a delicious, energetic, sweeping drama – surrounding and overwhelming…the next, as a consequence of the labelling, it was in a box, literally, limited to a small TV screen (in the dream) being watched from outside by something distanced and cut-off …the whole thing deprived of all its syrupy, mingling power. Waking up, the emergence of a bedroom and sunlight through curtains (but without the labels 'bedroom', 'sunlight', 'curtain' or even 'through'), and (thankfully) the full multidimensional, multisensory, surround-sound experiential was restored.

87. Reality is holey-ness

Worn, faded, flaking, degraded,
The ancient scrolls have lost their 'es' –
And all their meaning,
Through mass misreading:
The meaning of 'holy' is 'holey'.

Reality comes apart in the fingers
As soggy photograph.

Or as through magnifying glass –
All bulges and bends
And bursts into flames
And wilts and disintegrates
Just the same.

88. The word 'de-liberate' has a lot to say

The word 'deliberate', in its polysemy (its multiple meanings), is full of insight. In its normal usage, the word has two meanings. Firstly it means 'intentional', doing something *deliberately*; and secondly it means to 'think carefully', to ponder with *deliberation* (OED). Clearly these two meanings are connected. A 'deliberate act' is supposed to be the consequence of 'deliberation' as opposed to, say, 'instinct', in which there is no, or purely unconscious, thought preceding action.

Leaving this be for the time being, let a third rendering of this term 'deliberate' be introduced. Although the word is, contemporarily at least, not used in this way, the insertion of a hyphen reveals 'de-liberate' - the removal of liberation.

This third meaning casts light on the first two meanings. What is meant by 'intention', by 'being deliberate'? It implies the existence of certain bodies called 'free wills' or 'individuals' that have the power to choose, and that are therefore responsible for their actions. And what is meant by deliberation, by careful consideration? It implies thought that is purposefully undertaken by one of these 'free wills' that is therefore responsible for the act.

As has been stated and restated in this text, it is this very concept that there are such things as 'individuals', as 'free wills', that is the sense of enslavement, of de-liberation. Suddenly, there is an 'I' who is responsible, to blame, guilty, for everything this body does, every way these thoughts and feelings form and move, whose entire existence must be either the chronic justification, rationalisation and reassurance-craving of 'the victim', or the blustery, belligerent, bombastic self-affirmation, self-promotion, of 'the victor', the egotist.

In reality, there is no 'deliberate' in any of the three senses of the word. That which is labelled 'deliberate' and misconstrued as relating to something called 'will', is in fact pure chance. One thought appears - for instance, 'Shall I continue reading this book or shall I go and watch paint dry?' - another thought follows - 'I would much prefer to continue reading this, it is infinitely more stimulating' - and then maybe an action comes about - staring into space, perhaps, dribbling, skipping several pages to the next 'sex fix', or whatever. In all of this, where is there 'choice' or 'a chooser'? There are just events taking place - thinking, feeling, activity - without any controller, without any stabilizers attached.

89. Nondual expression is contradictory

Nondual expression is very often contradictory. One says 'When awakening happens...' one moment, and the next moment one says 'there is no awakening; all there is is awakeness'. One says 'there is no time' and then, 'Four months ago, when it first became apparent that there was no time'!! One says, "There is no space, no such thing as space" and then one says 'And that is seen 'over here', while that same seeing is overlaid by beliefs "over there". One says, 'There is the appearance of colours and forms' and one says, 'There is no colour, no form, nothing'. One says, 'There is no one here', and then one says, 'Today when I was going to the shops to buy some eggs...' This contradiction happens only because words describe the limited. Words describe something located somewhere. Even if the word is 'everything' there is a tendency for the mind to make an abstraction of this, cognising a symbol or a structure or a movement or an image that is supposed to represent 'everything'. So attempting to talk about nonduality is a bit like dancing on hot coals. Everywhere you tread, each word you choose, each phrase, each subject, is dangerous, is misleading, is conducive to perpetuating the idea of separative selfhood and all its difficulties and hurtfulness. One dances on coals; one dances to keep moving away from words, to keep eluding thought, while at the same time, leaping right onto fresh problems, fresh structures.

Having said all this, there are ways in which words are wonderfully expressive of nonduality.

90. One cannot 'be' with oneness; there is only oneness

A friend of mine sees a teacher who advocates technique. And this friend says to me, 'I don't see why technique necessarily enforces the sense of 'me'. I cannot argue with him, because, in a way, there is no reason why technique must generate the sense of a 'me'. The fact is technique simply happens, appears in consciousness, or doesn't. This may or may not be accompanied by the belief that there is someone there instigating the occurrence. So meditation and so forth is absolutely fine, immaculate, and this teaching here does not discourage it. Funnily enough, and all the same, this passage finds itself moving towards a natural critique of technique. This teaching does not discourage method the same way it doesn't encourage it. And the reason this is happening is that it is the sense that something needs to be done, whether that be to start meditating or stop, that engenders the erroneous belief that enlightenment is somewhere else, that there is something, a me, that isn't yet enlightened. There is no 'me' and there is only enlightenment. In a way, technique *is* being discouraged here, but only in the sense that not practising a method is a subtle way of practising the method of not practising, all of which tends to foster the blinding propaganda of enlightenment: that there is such a thing, that some people have it, and one day I might too. Technique can also encourage the topsy-turvy sense of 'I am experiencing oneness'. One often hears 'masters' saying 'move into this', 'play with this', 'stay with this' and 'be with this'. The whole thrust of this is highly misleading and just plain mistaken. It is far more helpful to say that 'this', oneness, experiences being you, or at least experiences what is being experienced, that may include a sense of 'self' (that is the product of misinformation). The source appears as the appearance. Seeing things 'this way round' is a far more helpful and potent pointer to seeing the nature of reality. The actual raw fact, however, is that the source and appearance are the same oneness; there is no hierarchy, no difference, no 'way round'. To suggest that one can 'be' or 'not be' 'with this', this oneness, is just daft; that which is imagined to be 'not with this' is actually wholly and solely 'this' itself.

91. The only fact there is, is called 'presence'

The only fact there is

Is called 'presence'.

What is meant by this word?

Some say

'She has real presence',

Meaning, 'She is a bold, charismatic person'.

But this is not 'presence'.

Boldness and charisma may be present, yes,

But only in the same way

And to the same degree

That timidity, blandness

And this book in these hands

Are present.

Presence is

'What is'.

Presence is

'This'.

Presence is always present here,

Present there,

Present everywhere…

This sense of being,

This sense of something:

Presence is all -

The indivisible -

And 'presence' is what you are called.

92. Sex is a simple, one-pointed impulse

(When Randy),

> If it's not a thing
> One can stick one's dick in,
> One doesn't give a dickens
> About 'it' or 'him'.
>
> The same with 'abstaining':
> Heaven is for him
> Who dislikes dirty linen,
> 'Tis his infinite Dick Inn!
>
> This isn't sinning,
> There is no such thing.
> Just the endless filling in of
> A being endlessly thin.

93. All there is, is dislocation

That which is called 'oral communication' is very much like ventriloquism, or the lip-synching found in pop videos, where one or more bodies 'mime the words'. The propaganda is that a somebody, or even just a body, is speaking. This is wrong. Speaking is speaking, and, incidentally, lips are moving. To shake up the conditioning one could say that speaking is moving the body, rather than the body forming speech, but actually this is just as false: the fact is, sound is sounding, and a body is moving. That's it.

There Is No 'Mastery'; All Is Love

94. All is love

All is love.

Does this sound banal?

Navel-gazing

Hippy drivel?

Consider what 'love' is.

Love is the collapse

Of all sense of form

(My angst-ridden past,

My ugly face,

That always comes last

Or first-place;

My anxious future

An endless rat-race;

Daunting and vast

Is 'this world' I must face).

Love is the collapse

Of all of this,

A lovely lapsing

Into sensual bliss

In the lap of my lover,

Her skirt is the sea,

A silky embrace

Lapping all over me…

This elapses eternally,

This sets 'me' free.

For here, there is no 'reality' -

All form is but pure fantasy.

Nothing so hard

As 'a place' or 'a face',

Suppleness, subtlety

Is 'time and space'.

95. On lovemaking, and how 'Mastery' and 'Guru' are absurd terms

Lovemaking is everywhere. By 'lovemaking' I mean an energetic doing culminating and collapsing in blissful surrender. The child spins on the spot, spins and spins, until he drops... the footballers sprint all over the place, 'til the ball is deposited in the net, the explosion of jubilation and then the collapsing, panting, in each others' arms... the mountaineer traverses treacherous, torturous terrain, to flop with ecstasy at the summit, and weep, on return, in her lover's arms... the lovers are horrid to each other – arguing, denying affection, being critical and cruel... only to show the full force of their care for each other, when it breaks down in tears and cradling.

The examples are endless. The struggle, the industry, of 'making' something, of doing, only for the wonderful falling into love once the doing is done. It is the struggle of Purgatory – to make The Kingdom come.

Some claim that when enlightenment emerges, the 'making' bit disappears and there is only love. Heaven, Paradise, is everywhere; Earth, with all its struggle and strife, a bad dream awoken from. This is so and not so; it is a 'yes and no'. Yes, it is known that there is only love, but this revelation perceives that struggle is love struggling: fight, conflict, aggression - all this is pure love. What is going on always is oneness, love, playing the game of division and conflict - appearing as different objects labelled 'people' debating, struggling, killing each other. Enlightenment sees that it is really not a case of love being made at the end of effort, but that effort and relaxation, harmony and disharmony, are all made of love, is all love-making...making itself into something. This seeing may be behaviourally reflected where this is seen: for example, it is noticed that the alternating binary mechanism of 'struggle' one moment, 'collapse, relaxation and celebration', isn't so much the reality for this body and mind anymore. Yes, as the misleading teachings proclaim, enlightenment experiences that love, bliss, orgasm, fulfilment, is everywhere, always and everything. It doesn't get switched off in effort and switched on in the end of effort. It lies not in end-gaining, or rather it does, but it is everywhere else also, and so it is endless and there is no 'end' to 'gain'. So yes, life seems much less of a struggle. Satisfaction is no longer somewhere else to be earned, achieved. This is the greatest hour. This is the absolute pinnacle, and it is infinite. But the other thing that has been noticed is that because love is known to be everywhere, struggle can happen with experiencing of love being right there, right here. For example, some teachings talk of 'the master' being a something that, because there is a seeing of oneness and love in everything, is therefore infinitely caring, eternally patient, boundlessly kind. This is just daft. 'The master', seeing that everything is already and invincibly immaculate, may absolutely revel in the atrocious, wanton freedom of this, by carelessly disagreeing with everything anyone suggests, impatiently interrupting questions before they have even begun, unkindly cracking bawdy jokes at the sensitive ego's expense. Infinite love is care and carelessness, patience and impatience, kindness and jubilant violation. It is non-selective, unconditional.

As a brief appendage, let it be said that the word 'master', as a label for the awakened perception, is one of the most stupidly conceived terms there has ever been. Awakening is the seeing that there is absolutely no mastery, no control, no guidance, on any level, anywhere. There is just ungoverned, unchallenged, unshaped anarchy. There is nothing called 'will', let alone a 'free' one. There is just consciousness, that is undivided, formless and nothing – it can have no influence on anything. It is syrupy. Funnily enough the term 'The Master' generates anything but the impression it should. It is a colossus, the Big Daddy to end all Big Daddies, the thing that could never put a foot wrong, that is superhumanly in control of everything. The Control Freak to end all Control Freaks. Yes, there is perfection, but that is only ever the case, before and after the seeing of it, in tripping over a stool, the stubbing of a toe and in talking very slowly and wearing pseudo-Indian or even real Indian clothes.

'Guru' is perhaps an even more absurdly ill-conceived term. It means 'the destroyer of illusions': the absurd thing about this being that the only illusion there is, is the idea that there are such things as 'someones', called, for example, 'gurus', 'disciples' or 'destroyers'. The term casts the very illusion supposedly being destroyed! There is no destroyer. There is no one. But the destruction and creation of the illusory can and do come about, by themselves.

96. There is nobody to save, and nothing to change (an email)

Hi Phil,

During the few weeks before it became clear that everything is what I am, I had some of those dramatic meditative kind of experiences - you know, feeling really blissful and full of grace and all that - and during these I would often fantasize about being a communicator of awakening; and pictured myself as a highly intelligent, noble, articulate and charismatic person, speaking before a captivated audience, naturally populated by gorgeous adoring females.

And then it became clear that 'this is already it', 'this has only ever been consciousness appearing', and there was no motivation to communicate whatsoever... because it is obvious that everything is already perfect, nobody is in need of being saved or of changing at all.

97. 'I' is a mirage

Is there something in this eye?
It looks glazed, preoccupied.

Ah, now I see.
It's that 'someone' called 'vanity',
'Self-consciousness' or 'me'.

Have a quick blink,
Rub those eyes,
Stretch those limbs,
Yawn open-wide.

Now leave bed,
To the bathroom go;
Lift those lids,
Deposit that load...

And now is the time...
Now is the time...

Mirror, mirror - let it be seen!
That secret someone known as 'me',
To the edge of the eye, or so it may seem,
Isn't there - is made of dream.

98. This mind's been washed (written days after enlightenment)

It looks like
This mind's been washed,
Wiped, buffed, and polished!

And hung on the line to dry by the ears,
So they hear -
Loud and clear.

Clear as a sparkling brass trumpet!

And all is so near, so near - SO NEAR!!

Ice in a glass!

Lily in a vase!

Newly clipped grass!

(Clichéd, yet)
So fresh, so vast...

The taste of toothpaste,
The touch of two waists

Ridden with energy, hidden as dynamite!
Fire of Infinity - fires the finite!

Well obviously, naturally, of course, aha!

Ha Ha!
Eureka!
Ha Ha!
Ha Haaaa!

99. No one is reading this book

'Prior to enlightenment', strange, trippy seeings, for example, the TV bulging and shrinking, somehow 'registered' in a way that doesn't happen anymore. Before awakening, the thought would happen, 'Wow, look at this…this is it…if I can keep this going then…' It is as if that which used to say that kind of thing, think in that manner, has simply gone, vacated the premises. Any kind of nugget-like formation in consciousness, like that kind of homely, personal thinking - me talking to myself, and also, for example, the looming, glaring, claustrophobic feeling of self-consciousness, and the experience of being a radiantly special, popular, 'real somebody', say on a particularly good night out - all of this is symptomatic of the self-believing state of pre-enlightenment. After enlightenment, there is no formation anywhere, or at least the habit of forming (things like selves, fear, the future, guilt, objects) begins to die. So, now, with the TV bulging and shrinking, this was just happening and registering nowhere. There was no one seeing it; there was just that. Contraction, formation, is a rare occurrence now, it has become an abnormal state, but when it does come about its rarity and comparative potency make it stick out like a sore thumb, and the awareness this generates tends to disperse it, there and then.

My current feeling is that this is a good way of measuring how far the seeing of oneness has been embodied, adjusted to. The less there is form and forming, the more settled and complete is the adjustment process. Immediately 'after awakening' there can be periods of imbalance where dense form sits alongside light formlessness, and sometimes 'syrupiness'. This can feel a bit funny, perhaps a little like lumpy custard? An incongruous landscape of both rugged outcrops of ice and great streams of moving water springs to mind.

100. This is a kind of 'Magic Eye'

This is a kind of 'Magic Eye'.

First notice

That your current way of looking

Sees a world that is an object,

Made up of lots of separate objects:

This is a notice over here,

You are a body placed over there;

There is a sort of space between us

And there is ground beneath your feet.

Now notice that all these apparent objects,

Including the body you believe is seeing the objects,

Are experienced, seen,

By something that is not the body,

Or any object.

The body,

That which you have believed to be 'the experiencer',

Is experienced…

Just as weight, papery-ness,

And these little black squiggles here are.

Suddenly

Reality is no longer

Solid and separated.

All is floating,

Suspended,

In this single consciousness.

'Me', this notice,

'You', that body looking at me,

The space between us,

And the ground below,

Are all made of a single consciousness;

There is only consciousness,

Oneness.

This Is Not 'An Excuse'

101. Apology, repentance and forgiveness are delusive and destructive

In perhaps every culture that has ever existed apology, repentance and forgiveness have been considered valuable virtues. But they are only valuable if some virtue lies in blame, guilt, vengeance, reactivity, repression, self-righteousness, low-esteem, masochism, sadism, general pervading psychological misery and the belief in bondage. Apology, repentance and forgiveness only confirm and compound the propaganda of responsibility. Apology may temporarily relieve guilt, and forgiveness resentment, but over all, this whole generic activity only compresses and hardens the dogma of choice, which holds imaginary entities, called 'people', accountable for totally chance events, causing belief in, and neurosis over, great burdensome mountains of judged actions of the past and looming ghostly mounts of potential slip-ups and disgraces to come.

Paradoxically, it is this very psychological strain, stemming from the oppressive belief in responsibility and blame, that brings about so many of the atrocities considered blameworthy.

Knowing that there is no responsibility is freedom. Then you can't go wrong, ever. What a relief; what a freedom this realisation is. See that that which is called choice is just the chance favouring of one point of view or course of action over another - thought moving of its own accord. Know that there is no navigator shaping this rise and fall of sensations, and this freedom is yours. You *are* this freedom.

102. This is not 'an excuse', there is nothing to excuse (an email)

Hi Nai,

I'd better be honest from the outset and tell you that today I am writing out of a purely gratuitous desire to entertain myself. Please forgive me! Of course, I am going to talk about nonduality, because you are one of the very few people who at least pretends to listen!! I was thinking about this yesterday and I thought how much it is like walking around with a really exciting secret that everywhere I go I am continually reminded of... and so I am naturally bursting to tell everyone about it, but mostly people either disbelieve it, aren't interested or don't get it (apart from when they do). My anxiety is that people (that means you) think I am trying to convert them to something, to some belief or faith or way of thinking... when it has nothing to do with any of this. It's much more like me saying, 'Check out that firework display over there', or 'Take a couple of these and the room will go all bendy'!!

I was thinking about the word you used to describe how all this nonduality business seems to you; you said it seems like an 'excuse'. I thought it was a very good word for thinking about it. When it is seen, it is realised that you are totally 'excused' of everything; and so is everybody else. You are excused of the dream of 'you'. I am sure this is what Jesus meant by 'redemption' and 'salvation' (though I doubt most Christians would agree - they are big on 'responsibility', 'free will' and all that).

But the thing is, Nai, making excuses doesn't really come into it. If things are seen as just happening, without any responsibility anywhere, it is a very accepting, understanding, forgiving perception. Can you see that? You kill my mother and I see that it was just a happening, that the thought arose to kill her, and the action followed... but that no one caused it. Then of course there is sadness and perhaps anger happening, but these things flow in and out far more easily and naturally if it is just realised as an arising in which everything and everyone is excused.

In actual fact, it seems to me that it is the belief in volition that gives birth to excuse-making. You turn on *Big Brother* and there are just countless examples of people trying to justify, rationalise and excuse themselves in order to deny the actual guilt they feel... as a result of the belief that there is a somebody there who has or is free will. I know you must have noticed it. It's really clear in the kind of person who spends the whole evening telling you about how amazing they are and all the amazing things they have done - it's all an extension of this. And people do it to each other; you say 'Guy, you're so lovely', and I say 'Naomi, you're the most fantastic person I've ever met'! Of course, I actually think this (well more or less!!) but I know that no one is responsible for it: that feeling 'proud' or 'flattered' about this would be the response of misconception.

Do you get it? If I excuse myself for killing somebody (although really excusing doesn't come into it because it is seen that there is no one there to excuse, or no one to blame in the first place), I also excuse the victim's relatives for their hatred of me, the judge and jury for convicting me, the executioner for hanging me and the politicians for producing this system (although again the reality is that there is no one, no choice-centre called 'executioner', 'politician', or 'me', to blame or excuse, to kill or be killed).

All this blaming and justifying and making excuses and guilt and denial etc: you know, Bush did this, Blair is guilty of that, and Bush and Blair say 'No no no! We're great, we made the best decisions in the world ever... but that nasty Saddam chappy, *he's* the fount of evil'. All of that just comes to an end, or gradually drops away.

Hope you enjoyed this even if only a little bit. I don't want you to believe me, but I would love for you to see the reality of all of this because then someone would 'get' me and then this terribly nagging secret might stop screaming at me! I'm glad it does though.

Lots of love to you Naomi,
Write anything you like to me,
Guy

103. Choice is a prison, not freedom

Where is the freedom in 'choice'?

Choice is burdensome

The sense that something

Has to be done.

'Choice' is a prison.

Even if I elect to make no decision

This is a choice,

This is my voice,

My decision.

Seeing that there is no choice or chooser,

No responsible body,

No winner or loser,

Free I am of this tiring endeavour

Then simply I am

Without purpose or plan.

104. The only fact there is, is 'There is this'

Whenever this text strays too far from the simple, direct acknowledgment of 'this', wherever it becomes discursive, it curls up and dies. There is not the energy to propel it. Even this, this writing about writing about this, is too far removed for much more self-sustenance than these few feeble lines of text. So let the simple acknowledgement of 'this' be now expressed. Wherever you go, whatever your surroundings, your feelings and your thinking, this will always and only ever be made of an awareness that is what you are. You perceive all that is perceived, including that which has been labelled 'you'. It seems strange that this very obvious thing has been so universally, with very few exceptions, overlooked. Let it be explained again. What is the foundation? What is the undeniable? There is something, isn't there? There is *this*. One cannot deny that there is something going on - call it 'consciousness', 'awareness', 'being', 'presence', 'existence' - whatever feels right. So this is the foundation, this is the only undeniable. Immediately, the mind leaps from here. It says, 'Yes yes, that's obvious, but if you stop there, at such a simple, basic thing, you get nowhere. Do you think science and technology and psychology and art and all the wonders of modern civilisation would have come about if such ponderous thinking had been tolerated? Why state the obvious?' Let this mode of thinking be answered. Yes, there is science and technology and great complexity of thought, but have you noticed how pervasive unhappiness and discontent are - perhaps as much as ever? I don't know for sure, but I think that in all the centuries of human existence misery has not decreased and happiness has not increased. For the simple fact that you who are reading this are to some degree dissatisfied and fearful (unless you are not, in which case you probably aren't reading this, because it has no function for you) please humour the remainder of this brief passage.

So, there is this. There is. Isness is. Formulate it however. From this simple, obvious-stating fact, observe that one aspect of this 'thisness' has been the labelling of certain appearances as 'me'. But it has gone further than this. This labelled 'me' is so convincing, that instead of seeing that there is this in which senses of 'me'

198

and 'not me' may or may not arise, there is the belief that the foundation is a 'me' 'over here' looking out at a separate world 'over there'. Can you see the fallacy of this? I, that am perceived or felt in consciousness, and 'the world', that is also perceived, are not primary. They are appearances in consciousness that is what I am, what being is. This is the totality of what is being said here, and it is totally logical, sensible, intelligent. There is nothing secretive or suspect about it; it is as plain as this book in your hands. Perhaps it is too obvious; so plain it is overlooked.

The great news, though, is that this is always less than one step from being realised; infinitely less than one step! This is it already! How can it not be? There is only consciousness; there is only 'this' – nothing can be outside of it. You have arrived; you have never left. You are fast asleep in the Garden of Eden, dreaming of a dark and fearful place you call Earth, but now I, this text, am whispering in your ear and reminding you of where you are, what you are. Sometime you will awake, and see there was only ever Eden. The Fall was but a Falling Asleep, a forgetting of what you are, a dreaming of where you aren't. Here you are! This is it! Hooray!

Some 'Deictic-Imaginative' Attempts At Revealing The True Nature Of Reality

105. A 'deictic-imaginative' attempt at revealing what is the case, always

Here is a 'deictic-imaginative' attempt at revealing that which is the case, always. Right now there is vision: a sense of you, perhaps, in the foreground, this book here in the middleground, and the other side of a room, perhaps, a view out of a window, or something else, in the background. Now imagine that a fire is spotted. First see that is all around you, all around this body sat here from the furthest periphery of vision, all horizons, to right in front of you and beside you. It is a fierce red and it crackles and burns and smoulders. It obliterates all sense of space because it is everywhere, there is nowhere it is not. Now notice your eyelids are aflame, and your eye, and your body, and everything that is the sense of 'you': the feel of 'I am' or 'I am this'. Now there is just fire, nothing but fire. There is no 'here' and 'there', no 'you' and 'not you', no 'inside' and 'outside'. There is just fire, just fierce, surging, plunging redness. That fire is called energy. That fire is called what you are. It is what you are made of; it is your real body stripped of all its deceptive appearances of flesh and landscape and objects and perspective, houses and villages and nations and planets. You are the consciousness that is everywhere, everything, everyone, all. You burn the towns and villages to nothing. The whole universe burnt through in an instant. You are the fire in which life burns. You are life burning. It has always burned; the fire has always been there, been here.

106. Imagine water – pure water without limit

Imagine water -

Pure water without limit,

With nothing in it

Or outside of it.

Not even motion

Nor shape, nor shade.

No cavity

No gravity -

Just water,

Pure water without limit -

Nothing in it

Or out of it.

107. I am 'the hardest button to button'

There is a song by The White Stripes called *The Hardest Button To Button*. This is one of the best metaphors for selfhood I have ever come across. I am the hardest button to button because however much there is bragging and asserting, defending and justifying, however much effort is put in, there is still no one here, this is still purely the activity of impersonal, characterless consciousness. One tries over and over again to make that button appear through the buttonhole, to make self a real, stable, forceful reality, this effort to be a someone, a free will; but it just won't happen, because it is a lie. There is only consciousness, trying to believe it is a person, but deep down knowing there is no one.

108. Biography

No biography is written here.

Biography is the fullest delusion there is.

Delusion is fine

But it is counteractive to the pointing out of how things really are

(Going on here).

Biography describes a distinguishable, singular something it calls

'A someone'.

It talks in terms of 'a body', 'a mind' and 'a life'

As well as 'birthplace', 'family' and so on.

This narrative has no interest in perpetuating such myths.

In fact, its singular concern is the extinction of all such fictions.

There is no 'body' or 'mind', let alone any 'life' or 'person'.

Look: where is this thing that has been labelled 'you' or 'me'?

Right now, this very moment - where is it?

There are colours and shapes,

A sense of perspective,

Sounds and feelings

And so on.

But where in any of this is 'a person'?

There is no such thing.

The fact is: there is no such thing as 'things'.

There are no objects,

There is just supple, fluid impression

Appearing and disappearing.

To talk about an object called 'Guy Smith'

Who one day got or became

Another object called 'enlightenment'

Is nonsensical,

Mistaken.

109. My biography

Here is my biography,

Obituary, biology,

The whole world's being and history:

This is it – this ink is me.

(Psyche [call it psychopathy],

Marrow, trim or gristly,

Blood and bloodline ye olde,

Does not exist, is purely 'this'.)

Heaven
Is Here

110. Existence is absolute reliability appearing as total unreliability

Today a friend of mine said, right out of the blue (he was editing his CV at the time), 'In a harrowing and turbulent world, you are one thing I can rely on'. He was both right and wrong. That which is labelled 'Guy', the body that is continually ageing and will die, the thoughts that are in perpetual flux, the emotions that change in an instant via the tiniest trigger, is the most unreliable thing in existence (joint first with everything else that exists). Guy is so changeable that actually there is not a single ounce of permanence, of continuance, that can be called 'Guy'. This is the essence of unreliability. At the same time, what I am, the being that is, *is* the only thing to rely on. It is unchanging, infallible, infinite. It is the best of friends, as it is always there, eternally accepting, infinitely patient...it wraps all around you and is you. Unknowingly, what my friend gave expression to was the exposure of the fundamental misconception of his Christian faith. Christians believe that *specifically* Jesus, a *particular* body that lived and died, was Christ and God, something eternal and infinite. The truth is, Jesus, the temporal, formal somebody, was as mortal, limited and 'sinful' as the pet dog. What is meant by 'Christ' is the space-less, timeless nothingness that is never born, never dies, and is what you are. It is *this*. So the 'I' of the words 'before Abraham was, I am' and the 'me' of 'the only way to the father is through me' have nothing to do with a historical somebody called 'Jesus of Nazareth' and everything to do with that out of which all words and all things arise, always. It is this, right now: there is only this. Where is there, what is there, that isn't presence?

111. The only 'location', the only 'period', is 'this'

Do you believe in Planet Earth?

It is talked about so much…

Perhaps you think there *must* be such a place?

If so,

You probably believe this notice,

And the body reading it,

Are situated 'there'.

They are not.

This notice is a message

Direct from the essence of reality,

Shouting:

THERE IS NO SUCH PLACE AS PLANET EARTH.

Look -

Where is this 'planet' you keep talking about?

See -

There are just colours, impressions, appearing and dissolving.

This place has been called

'The Kingdom of Heaven' -

But it is not really a place.

It is the Nowhere and Nothing

Appearing as impressions,

Empty impersonations.

112. Words objectify; objectivity is illusion

Words tend to project the sense of an object

That is something separate.

For example,

If I say the word 'chair'

You don't think 'I am chair' or 'me, chair' -

You think 'chair' is a something that is somewhere else

To 'where and what I am'.

Likewise,

When a set of words (often labelled 'Jesus')

Say the word 'Heaven',

It is immediately assumed

That something and somewhere else is being talked about.

Consider what is said about 'Heaven'.

It is infinite, it is eternal, it is fulfilment and it is home.

What is the case right here, right now?

There is existence, there is a presence called 'life' or 'this'.

This sense of seeing and reading this notice

And of a body doing this -

All of which is sensed,

Made of sensing.

Always present,

The substance of all presence,

This sensing is 'infinite' and 'eternal'.

The greatest familiarity,

It is your home and family,

And perfect,

Infinite fulfilment.

113. Writing nondualistically can be full of self-sustaining zing

This textual expression of nonduality is a singular, peculiar thing. All other forms of verbal output progressively tire this mind and this body, but not nonduality. Seeing the oneness that is everywhere, everything, is like a good bath: one feels soothed, relaxed, opened, energized. So writing this, writing about seeing that, puts attention on that, and so the relaxation, the soft energetic lightness, is here. So this is basically effortless. It writes itself. This is actually the same with any literature, but because this kind of expression constantly reminds the body incidentally sat in front of the computer-screen reading the expression as it happens of this fact, the body doesn't get caught up in the illusion of having anything to do with the words appearing, and so it just chills and enjoys! This body has spent the best part of eight years 'trying to write a book'. It is only now the impossibility of this has been realised that a book is finally appearing, writing itself (incidentally, the intended, unrealised book was to be a novel). I have a feeling that if the intention to write a novel again happens to arise, the output towards this will be similarly laborious and 'minimalist'. There is a certain pure *zing* to this direct expressing of oneness that is incomparable.

114. I never experience(s) anything (an email)

Dear Sam,

The short answer to your kind enquiry is, I am well, happy, more serene and content than ever, feeling like 'I know where I am going', and in no way miffed with my much loved Chinese friend who emails me no more infrequently than I email him.

The long and more 'right' answer is to say that most of the time there is no sense of anyone being here anymore. What this involves is very hard to explain. One thing is that there is a certain invincibility about it; there is no one who can get hurt, be left alone, be rejected and so on, no character left; so there is a kind of fearlessness. It's so difficult to explain. I could say 'Waking up in the morning there is an awareness of a body, of a bedroom, of daylight, thoughts and so on, but no demarcation between any "me" and "not me" in this perception'. I am the consciousness in which everything is perceived, which is not located anywhere, not inside 'a body' or 'a life' or 'a world' or anything like that. Does that make sense?

Actually 'This had already happened' when I saw you in the summer, and as you could see, there wasn't any difference, right? There seems to be some gradual adjusting to this new perceiving going on, but it is very gentle and doesn't really have much to do with behaviour.

People don't like being advised by others but if you think asking me anything about what I've just said above would be relevant and helpful to you in any way, please feel free to ask.

Love,
Guy

115. Three ways of indicating the nondualistic nature of reality

There are only four ways of indicating, three of which are perfectly good ways of communicating what 'this' or 'nonduality' or 'consciousness' is. Yet, amazingly, with the odds seemingly stacked against it, the vast majority of teachers persistently opt for the one inappropriate option.

The first way of indicating 'that which is nondual' is to say 'Yes, that's it, yes that's it, yes that's it', to absolutely everything. The second appropriate option is to say 'No, that's not it, that's not it either, nor that', again, to absolutely everything. The erroneous but highly popular third option, on the other hand, says 'No, that's not it, but yes, *that* is it'. Instances of this misrepresenting include, 'No, masturbation isn't it, but sitting silently *is* it', 'yes, very slow, careful "tantric" sex is it, but no, "being idle" isn't it'.

The fourth and final way of indicating what is being indicated here is to say 'Yes and no, this both is and isn't it; it both is and isn't everything'. This is the most correct and frustrating answer possible.

(Attempting to express nonduality might be called the perfectionist's worst nightmare! Whatever is said, misleads. Or perhaps it is the perfectionist's dream-come-true: whatever is said 'is it'; it cannot be got wrong.)

116. Heaven lies in the twinkle of an eye

Heaven lies
In the twinkle
Of an eye,

Which is that glittering fountain,
Which life swims
Within.

117. It is words that keep the colossal illusion of 'The Universe' alive

Isn't reading an effort?

No wonder.

It is words that keep this colossal illusion of 'The Universe' alive.

Words create 'The Universe':

'In the beginning was the word...'

The word 'Universe' is read, for example,

And suddenly thought invokes some vast composite image -

A devilishly complex agglomeration of 'space' and 'stars',

'Planets' and 'gravitational pulls',

'Buildings' and 'people' and 'history' and so on.

There is no such 'Universe',

There is nothing.

What words do is make a reality that is lighter than touch

Appear as a dense, fragmented mass of 'things'.

The word 'book'

Creates the sense of a solid, distinguishable, autonomous
something…

But there is no such thing.

There is nothing.

There are colours, and shapes and feelings of

Weight and papery-ness and so forth

But all of this is but the appearance on consciousness

That is colourless, formless,

Characterless.

This Is Unimaginable And Unavoidable

118. Infinity, which is nothingness, is unimaginable and unavoidable

On several occasions my father has mentioned that a maths lecturer of his once asked his students to try to imagine infinity, and then to imagine nothing. From what my Dad said, it seems that the object of the exercise was to show how 'hard' and in fact 'impossible' this is.

If I had known at the time, I might have responded correctly as follows. By definition imagination is finite and therefore incapable of comprehending infinity. Imagination is the activity of stored mental imagery, remembered images, manipulated, rearranged into some 'new' forms that are, as all form is, necessarily finite, limited.

But infinity and nothingness *can* be seen, felt, or rather, they are the case, are what life is made of (and are the same oneness). Nothing happens outside consciousness. There is never any moment or place where this is not this. So this is infinite, changeless, omnipresent. There is nothing that isn't infinity, isn't consciousness. And since infinity is everything, it has no definition, is not a thing, and is therefore no-thing, nothing.

Your infinite self, you, infinity, is both unimaginable and unavoidable…you can't miss it!

119. The seeing of nondual reality renders certain concepts void

While nondualistic perspective reveals that there is absolutely nothing, in another way one can say that within the appearance *particular* concepts (*and not others*) become void. 'Avoidance' is one of these redundant concepts. As all there is is 'this', that which is labelled 'avoidance' is purely 'what is', and nothing is being avoided. Similarly, there is nothing that can be called 'laziness'. Laziness is supposed to be a variety of inactivity that is brought about by the 'irresponsibility' of 'a person'. But there is no such thing as 'a person', and so here is another redundant, false concept; and so there can be no 'responsibility', no 'irresponsibility' (yet more irrelevant, inappropriate concepts), and therefore no 'laziness'. There is no 'subject', no 'object', no 'choice', no 'volition', no 'self', no 'courage', no 'cowardice', no 'achievement', no 'success', no 'failure', no 'sickness', no 'health', no 'better' or 'worse', no 'progression', 'regression' or 'stagnation', no 'should', 'could', 'would'. And lots more! This compares to relevant, appropriate concepts such as 'red', 'sweet', 'sound', 'tingling'. One might make yet another category for more borderline concepts, for example, 'bread', 'breathing', 'sex', 'fast', 'fat'. 'Sex', for example, is more conceptual and less actual than, say, 'tingling' because 'what is', during what is labelled 'sex', is disconnected, dislocated happenings such as 'panting', 'tingling', 'wetness', 'swelling', and, with any luck, 'screaming'! There is nothing 'beyond' these or somehow 'in the middle' of these that can really be called 'sex'. But there are several disconnected, unrelated appearances, that can happen simultaneously, and be given a name, whereas 'avoidance', say, simply cannot happen.

120. Stream-of-consciousness, and nothing else

This is consciousness and never anything else. It's as simple as that.

The problem with the word 'consciousness' is that it suggests a something that is distinguishable from something else. The mind makes an abstraction, a symbol, an image of it – a definition in order that it has some way of comprehending, recognising and remembering it. But with consciousness, more than anything else (and actually - there isn't anything else), this is a mistake, an absolute misrepresentation. Consciousness is defined, so to speak, as having no definition, as being characterless and therefore unimaginable. Being everywhere and everything, it has every characteristic and no characteristic; it has no stable, structural quality or nature by which it may be defined.

In giving consciousness definition, mind generates the entire illusion. 'If there is something labelled as "consciousness", reasons the mind, 'there must be something that is not consciousness, outside of consciousness', in order that consciousness be defined, placed. Let this non-consciousness be termed 'matter'. With the concept of 'matter', the whole neurotic world of being a tiny, fragile, isolated mortal, traversing a huge, hostile universe, is born. Suddenly life is a succession of potential catastrophes, great monoliths of past guilt and future accountabilities, and the waiting and dreading of the coming end of this world.

The end of the world, the end of *that* world, is the greatest relief and joy there can be. See those great crucifixes you bear upon your back, dragging from this moment to that, year upon year, evaporate in an instant, as sunset clouds! Those immense stones you have heaved, constructing those pyramids, pointing to the heavens as your great bid, all of this reveals itself as but dream; and, waking, you see Paradise has never left you, you were here all along.

The brown apple-core in your limp left hand betrays the guilty narcotic: the Fall but the dropping of fruit from a tree, a falling asleep. The most convincing dream is the one in which you appear to wake up: Rock-A-Bye-Baby, tossed from the tree tops, burst through the foliage, to lie there sopping in your own juices;

your broken home in tatters about you, the cradle trashed, the bleeding womb that once was you; yes, the rudest of awakenings this seems. Suddenly, you are not the tree, for there she is, splayed before you, weeping for joy, at you, in your misery! Now comes the tiresome time of trying to re-climb her, striving to reclaim her, her attentions, her affections, from the clutches of the father. Inevitable failure. So, as Bye-Baby-Bunting, you go a-hunting, for some other she to heal this shame. Fortune and fame, more remedies for the pain, you make yourself the grandest tree, a home of your own, with you on the throne, as your security, your solidity. But still, you are not that. You are still alone. For the tree still stands in the garden, out of the window. She is just standing there, enjoying the sun. God damn it! You scratch your head and sigh. Why oh why? What is the point?

And that is life, more often than not. And that is fine, that is immaculate. In death it is known that the tree is once again all, has always been all, without any rejected fruits. The womb that is eternal and perfectly smooth, a black satin cushion gleaming of stars, is then what you are, and what you always are. A bottomless pit, is what you inhabit and is that which inhabits you. You are nothing. There is a lone yew, standing there alone, upon a hill, black and flat in pink twilight, and empty straights for miles and miles around... And beyond. Where have you gone? You were never there. Just the appearing and flourishing and withering of colours and shapes, sounds and tastes and touches... And then the eternal rest upon the satin cushion, curled up as an embryo, breathing so deep and slow... 'oh' is the sound you make... and '0' is all that is left.

This just meanders on...directionless 'poeticising': it has no point. Don't look for any. Only know you are this eternal meandering...going nowhere...getting nothing...only being... being, which is love.

121. There is no 'other'

I am one skinny mucker
Yet with just a little knife
I'm a much tougher fucker
Yet as soft as your wife
I slice like hot butter
Whenever you like
I could leave you in the gutter
In the dark, one night.

Don't be such a sucker
For this, these lies;
This is but inky splatter -
The 'threat' lies in your mind.
A dagger is no danger
Though bodies it may slice -
Then slicing by thy saviour,
The present presence of life.

Brother there is no 'other' -
No 'you' nor 'I', to 'kill' or 'die',
But one immortal mother is this,
This omnipresent life.

122. Selfhood is compelling and convincing (until it is examined)

Isn't it so compellingly convincing

That someone is saying these words?

That I am 'a someone', 'a narrator',

And not just ink?

Isn't it so compellingly convincing

That someone is reading these words?

That there is a 'you', a 'reader',

And not just consciousness

In which colours and forms

And sounds

And so on

Appear?

Sex And
The Text

123. Text appears as a sort of microcosm of reality

If this were a chore it wouldn't be here. Any effort at all and it would turn itself right off. Also, whereas those expressions labelled 'great writers' tend to advocate holding onto a good idea, writing it down the moment it happens, I notice that this kind of literary output improves on not retaining thoughts. Then they flow like a wellspring and either this body happens to be sitting in front of a computer screen and the words get typed and stored, or they disappear the moment they arise, without any sense of loss or concern. It seems that holding onto an idea, trying to retain it as memory for an imagined future typing session, only serves to block new thought, and, as it happens, when the time comes to type the memorised thought, it feels stale, burdensome and irrelevant, and doesn't get typed after all.

It strikes me that this writing here is a good metaphor for 'what is'. The text moves between two impulses. One, is the impulse to be daring, creative, active: as life, the appearance of things, multiplies and grows and stretches itself in all manner of weird and wonderful forms. Two, is the impulse to simply come home, out of the cold, out of the endeavour, and rest. This is the direct apprehension and expression of oneness, here now. One, is the appearance of playful endeavour, of life in all its drama; two, is that which appears, that which plays, just curling in the warm fire of its own being, its own snug body-heat. Both of these are one and oneness, and are what is meant by 'nonduality'.

124. On 'the spectacular transcendental experience'

During some months 'before awakening' some very spectacular, crowd-pleasing (i.e. mind-pleasing) experiences took place. The common denominator between them was the sense of a luminous something somehow 'behind' or 'inside' everything. Sometimes it was like a vast black river or a starless night sky - just kind of hanging there, watching everything, waiting. At other moments it was like a very bright and warm light had been switched on somehow inside consciousness, lighting up everything that is seen and also brightening all other senses, setting them on fire. Walking home from work today, this latter feeling of a sort of luminous presence presented itself once more, but in a much more ordinary, integrated way. It is just the norm now, and actually it has always been there. When it is first noticed, yes, of course, it can seem dramatic, radiant, spectacular, but now it is no more interesting, special or unusual than a chair, a radiator, the news.

125. Apology for the recent shortage of sexual-gratification

Reader, I must apologise. The frequent lust treats I sincerely promised you have been thin on the ground of late. To compensate, here is a highly-sexed, but also, I think, subtle and intelligent poem.

126. Big, fleshy jungle-sex can bring about certain disillusionment

Here she is, my clod of clay,
Squidgy, fleshy, on display;
Away she bends, this way and that way -
Eluding hands that roam astray.

Sometime later, rock hard she makes.
Arched back, as a model splayed.
Tugging a strap, a teasing thumb stays
Before that lump that bulges in weight…

Delay no more, please - no more play…
A foreskin folds, it rolls away,
The stripper peels free of her lingerie,
'I'm on the way now!' 'She's on the way…'

The clay is collapsed, all's unmade.
Limbs lie in dirty disarray.
One moment *I am* – so protrusive, so rude!
No more, I see, I shrink away…

127. There is no such esteemed personage as 'President Bush'

It comes apart in my fingers. It is the coming apart of my fingers. Consciousness cannot be seen or touched, because the seeing and touching, the eye and the hands, are consciousness themselves, consciousness itself. There is just consciousness, so it cannot be found. It is this, the seer, whether there is noticing or not. It might be described as 'magical' because it is simply present – as if by magic, without cause. It kind of floats or shines or flowers – it just is. There is no such thing as anything: try to move in the direction of that which you think is 'a thing' and it you will find there is nothing there; it will come apart, disintegrate, vanish. You think there is a something called President Bush? There is only an endless array of impressions (images of 'grey hair', 'a suit', 'a smirk'; sounds such as 'the war against terrorism...' and 'bang', for example), all of which add up to nothing. They don't 'add up': they are simple present, or not, as totally singular presences. There is only this supple presence - and what a relief when this is realised. Nowhere to go... nothing going anywhere... any way. Perfection, heaven at last and already!

(Having said that there is no President Bush one wonders if the world might fare a little better if there was? Bushes don't try and control everything - they just chill in the soil. So it would be 'Resident Bush', rather than President; just residing, rather than presiding: free from the illusion of government. That which believes it is called 'George W Bush' might be surprised and shocked to know that the greatest threat to his administration and the United States as a whole, is not that dream known as 'Al Qaeda', but the fact that there is no 'Bush administration', no 'United States', nothing solid, objective, 'real'. And certainly there is no 'presiding', nothing 'presidential' either. Governing, government, is an impossibility. Nobody has ever chosen to drop a bomb on anything; nothing has ever been banned by anybody. What actually happens is that the thought appears, 'dropping bombs is a good idea'. Then lips start wiggling and the sound 'droppingbombsisagoodidea' sounds again and again, at different pitches, in different tones, and more than likely the sounds 'no' and 'droppingbombsisnotagoodidea' too. And then, sooner or later, bombing happens, or it doesn't. Do you see? Where is the choice in any of this? You are powerless Georgie. You cannot kiss the girls and make them cry, but girl-kissing and then, incidentally, crying can take place, all of its own accord. The big boys came out to play (not 'Saddam' or 'Osama' - I mean 'Nothingness', 'Presence', 'Thisness') and Georgie Porgie runs away…into nothing.)

128. Titles are self-conscious, self-reflexive, self-creating things

Titles, as in names of 'books' and 'people', are inherently self-conscious, self-reflexive, self-perpetuating things. With the textual, what a title does is lump together several million little black squiggles, as if they were somehow one entity, one body, whose name is the text's title. A title says 'I am these black squiggles, what I am is called "a text" or "a book" and who I am, my name, is these words here, this title'.

A title is a good, clear example of dualistic thought. On the one hand there are the black squiggles, which are themselves, which are nothing but 'the black squiggles', and actually, there is no other reality, no 'self' beyond this. The title, then, embodies the misconstruction of selfhood: a title says, '*I am*, and who I am is this text; these black squiggles are not merely black squiggles, they are the great me, and who I am is an all pervasive, all-powerful, totally conscious and volitional Master of myself, which is also myself'. (Here the thought gets a bit confused and tangled up, but here I am hushing it up in brackets because his pride is so easily wounded! Deep down he knows he doesn't exist…). It would be appropriate, therefore, if this particular collection of black squiggles were proceeded by no title. Unfortunately, I fear this would inevitably extinguish the already tenuous chances of publication and sales!

129. This expression points to one fact in two ways

It is noticed that this expression attempts

To point out, describe and explain

Only one thing,

Actually, one 'no-thing',

In two principal ways.

First, it is simply noted that all is made of awareness.

There is nothing outside of awareness,

There is nothing that is not awareness.

With this seeing – all there is, is a singular oneness.

So, and secondly,

There are no separate 'things',

Be they (called) 'objects' or 'subjects'.

That which is labelled 'a book'

Is nothing but the colours black and white,

Squiggles and rectangles,

A sense of weight,

The appearance of sounds, images and feelings.

And that which is called 'me'

Is nothing but feeling, and the idea 'body',

And a zillion sounds, images and feelings

Falsely lumped together and labelled 'thoughts',

Falsely lumped together and labelled 'memory' or 'mind'.

There is no 'unity', no 'unit', no 'thing', in any of this.

Oneness Is The *Only* Certain, Provable Fact

130. Sleeplessness highlights the fact that volition is illusory

Confronted with sleeplessness the mind asks the question, 'How can I bring about sleep?' It feels a little agitated and anxious because, faced with the situation, it notices that it has exactly nil experience to draw from. It is a perplexing blank: 'But I'm sure I've managed this sleep business rather a large number of times before, haven't I?' The truth is, the mind has never once managed sleep. Sleep involves the falling asleep of the mind. That which wants to cause sleep engenders sleeplessness. It is a humbling realisation; the mind finds itself utterly impotent. In fact, this is the case in all things: thought simply goes this way or that, or falls asleep, with no one at the helm. It is a flag flapping in the wind, hanging in the calm.

131. Diabolical dramatisation of the dis-location of cause

The force took hold
And the force was she,
Silk tumbled in folds
Above the knee,
Of legs stretched bold
Yet carefree,
In sunset golden,
Syrupy.

Propped by the bole
Of the apple tree,
The force took hold
And the force was she,
Those shadowy boulders
Hung so heavy,
And swung in the cold
As she shuddered so slightly.

The twilight old,
Her form now silvery,
'Twas the gloom that stole
The dress from her body;
The darkness so whole
You could not spot me,
As the force stole in
And the force was she.

Now let me be bold,
Fair ladies of the jury,
This just unfolded,
It wasn't me.
The force took hold
And the force was she:
She was my pole,
My energy.

132. The seeing of oneness can prompt jubilant mischief

One element of what is taking place here, this verbal output, is mischief. Think only as far as the usually wholly unrelated rude poem insertions! You can spot this mischievous quality in what may be a disproportionately high percentage of expressions of this kind - look no further than Tony Parsons' dirty jokes! Prior to awakening, Guy was perhaps the least mischievous person you could meet. From his perspective at the time, mischief only endangered his principal life-purpose of trying to make everybody like him. But, when suddenly responsibility was seen to be a misconception, and immortality an axiomatic fact, I wouldn't exactly say that 'all hell broke loose', but it was certainly the case that, for a week or two, this apparent personality here was an appreciably more unpredictable, provocative, combative, irreverent, uncomfortable character to be around. I remember emailing a poor friend of mine a barrage of impudent jibes, just because suddenly I could, because I was free! This friend had been the person in the world I had most looked up to...and now this realisation...suddenly I was a rebel without a cause! Admittedly, we're talking amoeba-scale rebellion... yet at the same time it was an infinitely greater one than this no-body had ever staged previously.

To a degree, this kind of occurrence makes a mockery of the concept that enlightenment has something to do with 'being good'. This was the 'evilest' I've ever been!

133. An insincere, purely mischievous, ridiculous poem

If woman is God's gift to man,
He couldn't have chosen much better.
Legs a little longer, breasts fatter perhaps,
And perhaps just that bit wetter.

If woman is God's gift to man
(As I am God's gift to women),
The fact that the gift comes so well chosen
Shows God, without doubt, is man.

134. The direct, fresh expression: there is just indivisible thisness

In its hunt for variety, originality, freshness, its impulse to escape its own apparent repetitiveness, a text can forget to come back to the most direct, clear modes of expression.

But the direct, clear expressions do not express repetitiveness, even if the words (the ink formations) are the same shapes, and in the same order. What is being expressed is timeless, unmoving.

That infinite expression is this: this is oneness; there is just oneness. The apparent separateness of the object and subject is made of *and is* a oneness that is indivisible and is everywhere and everything. So there are no separate 'things', no such thing. 'What is' has been called many names amongst which 'this', 'is', 'presence', 'being', 'awareness' and 'oneness' are some or the least misrepresentative.

What is being said here is a truism. What is being said is that everything that is, is being. Being is being; 'isness' is 'isness': not exactly a controversial claim!

But when this unicity of being is felt, seen, realised (the realisation that all being is being, obviously), senses of separation, isolation, alienation, defensiveness, tend to drop away and this is a pleasant release and relief.

(A quick note: there isn't really any such thing as repetition. There is only infinity, timelessness, which is infinitely fresh. Repetition is an illusion projected by the mind addicted to naming, conceptualising and compartmentalising.)

135. Blackness is a metaphor for indivisible reality

Blackness is an incredibly potent metaphor. Everything sinking into colourlessness, darkness, blackness. Filling up with coolness. A river at night. Dark, cold, empty, nothing. A valley at night. Just collapsing, thinning, disappearing.

136. That which remains (untouched, unmoved)

'FREE SEX'

Is a phrase that grasps

Attention

With unparalleled

Aggression.

It is atomic.

In an instant one is grabbed by the words,

Gripped in arousal.

In this cataclysmic captivation,

Is there anything that remains untouched, unmoved -

Exactly as it was before?

The consciousness

Which registered the arousal

Is always the case,

Always 'there'.

It has no shape,

No form, no face:

For it is that out of which

Time and space

Are made.

137. Oneness is the only certain, provable fact there is

Oneness is the most obvious fact. Ten minutes ago a housemate of mine asked me if there was any evidence I could cite to prove the reality of what is being said here. There is *only* evidence for it! The evidence is unavoidable. We are not talking about scientific evidence here. Scientific evidence, which popular propaganda has come to equate with 'truth', is infinitely more suppositious, more removed, more shaky than nonduality. Who would question the fact that everything that appears happens in awareness? And who would question the fact that this awareness is indivisible and omnipresent, since there is nothing that appears without it? This is unquestionable. It is, in fact, the only absolute, concrete certainty there is. All else is inference, guesswork.

A common mental response to this sort of message is 'so what'. 'So there is awareness; this is awareness: big deal!' The 'big deal' about it, which is infinitely big and small, beyond scale, is that when this is witnessed and lived experientially, existentially, rather than simply stored as a remembered piece of knowledge, certain senses of neediness, dissatisfaction, fear and isolation, tend to melt away. If one knows oneself as an awareness that doesn't move or change, that is not of space and time and therefore cannot live or die, senses of being vulnerable, disposable, constantly threatened, those senses associated with being a limited form, a somebody, naturally come to an end. Likewise, senses of being impure, guilty, weak, inadequate, full of shortcomings, again associated with the idea of being a person, are annihilated in the light of knowing I am the changeless, formless, totally undefined purity that sees and knows everything that happens. The kind of language just used has the tendency to erect an abstract sense of something 'grand', 'deep' and 'intellectual'. In actual fact, it is the simplest, most innocent obviousness there can be. Look: everything, this book in these hands, these black squiggles, the thoughts appearing, the sense of a body, the sense of 'myself', the sense of 'room' in which this reading is happening - all of that is registering, appearing, in awareness. Is that fair? Is that clear?

Selflessness Has Nothing To Do With Altruism

138. Selflessness has nothing to do with altruism

One hundred per cent of the time, to the nearest per cent, the terms 'selfishness' and 'selflessness' are wildly misunderstood. Incidentally, this misunderstanding extends to the vast majority of expressions labelled 'nonduality'. The popular, pervading consensus is that 'selfishness' means 'doing everything for yourself, without regard for others'; and 'selflessness' means 'doing lots for other people'. Looking purely at the words, directly and simply, one can see that 'self-ish' means 'of the self' and 'self-less' means 'no self'. And what is it to be 'of the self'? It is simply the perception, which is a misperception, that reality is a divisible something composed of autonomous objects and subjects, the latter (subjects) being the focus of this term. This perception, however, bears absolutely no relationship to 'doing everything for yourself, without regard for others'. If there is the belief in selves, and the seeing of suffering, say, in Africa, there is every chance that activity will take place towards helping these 'poor souls'. And yet, this happens within the context of 'selfishness', perception which imagines the presence of 'selves', and there is nothing wrong with this.

And what is 'no self', 'selflessness'? It is the perception, the accurate, clear perception, that reality is that indivisible presence called something like 'awareness' or 'thisness'. And in this, there is no segregation into 'different things'; so there are no 'objects' and no 'beings', no 'selves'. And does this perception imply doing lots for others? Of course not! It is known that there is no such thing as 'others' or as 'anybody'. And what is perceived is that, by-and-large, these particular thoughts and feelings tend to be more sensitive to what this body needs than any other sets of thoughts and feelings. The thoughts and feelings labelled 'Guy' apprehend when that body that is also labelled 'Guy' is hungry and in need of food, better than, say, the thoughts and feelings labelled 'Michael Jackson'. And, in turn, the thoughts and feelings labelled 'Michael Jackson' know when the body named 'Michael Jackson' is in pain and in need of treatment, better than the thoughts and feelings labelled 'Guy Smith'. Now, it may be that the thoughts and feelings labelled 'the doctor' know how to treat the body labelled 'Michael Jackson' better than the thoughts and feelings labelled 'Michael Jackson', in which case, it would be advisable for 'going to the doctor' to happen. Similarly, the thoughts and feelings labelled 'certain African communities', for example, may be powerless to combat a particular malnutrition epidemic affecting bodies also labelled 'certain African communities', but aid from elsewhere may be able to help. But this is the case both where selfhood is imagined to be a reality and where it is seen that there is no self. Empathy and empathic action may or may not be present both before and after awakening; and everything is made of a substance that is without form, without imperfection, beyond pathology, psychopathy, health and happiness.

To clarify further, while it is certainly true that a false belief in selfhood can sometimes prompt obsessive over-protection of the body, thoughts and feelings being identified with (the belief that I am these mortal things leads to a drastic clinging to the means by which they, and hence the imagined 'me', might be sustained), it also happens, for example, that 'being altruistic and generous' gets identified with, and then anything will be done to sustain *this* activity.

139. Either compassion isn't enlightenment, or compassion isn't pity

A concept often associated with nonduality

Is 'compassion'.

This is a misconception.

'Compassion' is

'Pity inclining one to help or be merciful'.

Nonduality is beyond all inclination.

Nonduality is omnipresent, absolute;

It is no more 'here' than 'there'.

Absolutely, it is pity, help and mercy,

And so it is suffering, ruthlessness and atrocity.

This is it.

There is nothing that isn't it.

For the joy of gimmickry

One might call nonduality 'encompassion'.

Where compassion inclines, points as a 'compass',

'Encompassion' just *is*,

Beyond direction,

Discrimination or location.

Encompassing all, being all,

It is unmoved and unmovable.

An alternative approach to this

Is to offer a different rendering of the word 'compassion',

Which dispenses with the 'inclination' and the 'pity'.

Only then, is it correct to say that

'nonduality is compassionate'.

In being the knowing that there is no one

The awakened perception

'Mercifully' 'helps' expose the unreality

Of the imprisoning sense of selfhood…

And lets it vanish.

But this has nothing to do with sympathy.

If anything,

'Sympathy' nourishes the sense that there is someone 'there',

Someone 'in there',

In need of pity, help and healing.

Nothing could be less 'merciful' or 'helpful'

Than this -

This self-supporting

Teaching.

140. You are not reading this

What is it that is seeing this book here, these letters on this page? The conditioned, reflex answer is to say '*I* am seeing this book, these letters, this page'. Or perhaps one might say '*Eyes* are seeing this'. But what is it that believes this? Isn't it true that these senses of 'me reading this' and 'eyes seeing this' are seen or rather witnessed by something else? There is the experience of seeing this but also the experience of a sense of a somebody experiencing it, and the idea of eyes. But what experiences this? What experiences 'being' and 'seeing' and 'reading' and 'eyes'? There is something, though it can never be looked at, witnessed; it is the ultimate witness. Words always mislead where this is concerned, as this obviously is something that is without form, and the words 'witness', 'experiencer' and 'something' used above (for example) generate forms, senses of structure. Just see that with everything there is a placeless, formless awareness perceiving that. That's all that's being said here.

141. There is no logo

There is a book called *No Logo*

Which points out how businesses attract customers,

Sales, and profits,

By constructing and projecting attractive images, 'logos',

To represent themselves.

One of the points made is that the logo may be totally unrelated

To the product being promoted.

For example,

If a naked woman were pictured on the front of this book

It would attract horny heterosexual male customers

Regardless of the book's subsequent contents.

A carefully conjured dream, then, is selling the product,

While the product itself is irrelevant.

The book *No Logo* suggests that this kind of fantastical promotion

Induces somnolence.

No Logo is wrong.

The somnolence is already fully present, prior to the promotion.

For a logo to function, for it to come to life and have its being,

For it to blind and manipulate,

First it must be dreamt that there is a logo.

There is no logo.

When this is seen, when it is known that there are only unrelated colours,

Shapes, sounds and feelings,

The pull, the attraction,

Is dispersed,

Vaporised.

This is not a naked woman.

It is flat ink on a bit of paper.

The word 'sex' is not a feeling

Or a feverish compulsion.

It is three small black squiggles.

It is not that there *should* be no logo,

That logo obscures truth behind an appealing dream;

The truth is – *There is no logo.*

142. An imagined book called No Lego

When I heard of the book *No Logo*

I thought of writing a book called *No Lego*.

Lego conveys the sense that life is made of units,

Unifying to make bigger units.

Legoland is a land of materiality, physicality, body.

It is a thing, consisting of things.

The truth is,

There is no such thing as 'things'.

There is only 'this', which is indivisible.

The book I conceived of then pulled off the 'L' from 'No Lego',

The 'Learner' plate of the infant being conditioned,

To leave 'No Ego'.

In the imaginary 'world' of 'things' there are not only

'Physical bodies'

But also psychical or spiritual bodies called 'egos' or 'souls'.

The truth is,

There are no such things;

All there is

Is 'this'.

Now pull off the 'E' to leave 'No Go'.

Once it is seen that there is only awareness,

One knows there is no 'going',

And 'nowhere to go'.

As everywhere is 'right here',

Is the place called 'consciousness',

There is no 'here' and no 'there' –

There is only nowhere.

Finally,

Discarding the 'G',

What is left is 'No O'.

And 'NoO', 'no', is one great zero.

And that is what is.

There is no-thing

Appearing as the infinite,

One endless,

Placeless,

Pointless

Circle.

143. You don't have a pair of eyes, or even a head

This sense of 'being a somebody'

Is actually the sense of 'being two somebodies'.

Thought says things like

'Come on Guy, lets get this sorted'

Or 'I must make more space for myself'.

It is a conspiracy, a collusion, a cartel of two -

Between 'me' and 'myself'.

The following gimmick illustrates this in a different way.

Look in the mirror and notice how

The reflection and the imagined observer (the reflected)

Collude, conspire, relate.

Isn't there a sense of 'a team' or 'a close friendship' here?

It's a relationship, anyhow.

Now move so that the tip of your nose is upon the glass

And look straight into the reflection's eyes.

Continuing to look straight ahead,

Notice that to the left, or the right, or both

Is a ghostly 'half-reflection' that will not look at you.

It looks past you.

This is just a gimmick.

But perhaps it may inflict a gentle disturbance

Upon this sense of 'being a somebody'.

'This reflection will not look on me.

What's his problem? Doesn't he like me? Can't he see me?

Isn't he with me?

Then who is he?

And who am I?'

Someday it will be known that there is no one

Standing in front of the mirror,

And no one looking back.

Just glass,

Reflected light,

Colours,

The sense of a body.

That reflection,

That flat, empty image,

Is no more 'a person'

Than that which you call 'yourself';

You might say it is *more* of 'a person':

At least it has 'eyes' and 'a head'!

Do you believe

That which you call 'yourself' has or is these things?

Then look again!

144. The sense of 'being with yourself' points to the reality of oneness

The intimate, collusive sense of 'being with yourself' felt in separation, which is a relationship between two imaginary figures called 'me' and 'myself', witnessed, for example, when 'talking to yourself' or 'looking at yourself in the mirror', is so indicative. It indicates that there is consciousness (the first of these two imaginary colluding characters); and what consciousness is appearing as - a body, thoughts, feelings, behaviour, for example (the second 'me'). Consciousness sees a body appearing in a mirror and says 'That's me', and suddenly there is the schismatic, schizophrenic notion of 'I am the observer' *and* 'the observed', the appearance in the mirror *and* the seeing of that. This is the perception of separation. This separative perception, by the way, is what all religious movements eventually corrupt as, in terms of, say, 'matter' and 'spirit', 'self' and Self', 'identified' and 'enlightened'. And then you end up with 'individual selves', 'lives' and 'past-lives', 'responsibility', 'karma', 'holy ghosts' and 'gurus': all kinds of misconceived identities.

The truth is, there is only awareness. 'Matter' is a construct, a nonentity that can never be discovered. It is nothing but a dream. And when consciousness sees there is only consciousness, this relational, collusive sense of 'being with myself' tends to disintegrate. What remains in place of this is one of two things (and there may be an alternating between these). There can either be the sense that there is no character here, no 'me' whatsoever - only indivisible consciousness in which there are no things at all, nothing. Or there can be the sense of a character here, but that this character is a ghostly construct of the imagination, a playfully imagined sum of specific somatic, emotional, psychical and behavioural activities, and that he or she is made purely of a consciousness that is indivisible from all else. So, in both cases, it is seen that all is awareness.

On Textual
Hypnotism

145. Some incidentals surrounding this awakening (an email)

Hi Neera!

A long time has passed since we were last in touch. For my part, a good deal of that has been down to the very thing I'm writing to you about here.

I remember when I last saw you, in that noisy bar in London, you recommended to me that Roger would be a good person to contact if I felt that would be helpful. At the time I saw you, there had been the sense of a lot of 'shifting' going on...a lot of the time there was no one 'in here', and that felt dizzyingly light, chaotic, overbalancing and 'too much'. At other times it felt very calm and free. Soon after I saw you I went to the Citizens Advice Bureau about something and left feeling a lot worse than when I arrived. The lady I talked to basically seemed to think there was a good chance I would soon be massively in debt and quite possibly taken to court. (Thankfully, she was wrong, she misread the papers I showed her.) I remember walking home feeling very calm, that none of this was registering or impacting anywhere. And then, when I was at home, there was an enormously tight clutching in my stomach, and so I phoned Roger.

He didn't say much; he just encouraged me to 'pause', like we do at his meetings, and said that this simply 'restores natural functioning'. This pausing happened, and over the next few days I felt the clutching gradually softening, uncoiling and dispersing; and it felt like tender bruising for some time.

At the same time as this, and ever since, it has been clear and obvious that there is only consciousness. There is no 'me', as that which witnesses sensation is without character or quality; it is nothing and nobody. This has been put into so many different word-formations you have read, I don't think there is any point in me rattling on about it. What is clear, though, is that 'this is it'. It could not be any clearer; it is simply seen, known.

I didn't tell anyone about this for a long while because talking about it felt somehow 'wrong', inaccurate. To say that 'I am now awake' or 'awakening happened at the end of April' is just incorrect, and object-generating. I didn't know what to say!

I think I told you that I love writing, but at the same time I have found it impossible to write much. Every time I formulate a plan for, say, a novel or even a short story, I am totally turned-off by the prospect of actually having to produce the great mass of text.

Anyhow, since awakening, a great deal has been typed by these fingers. I think this is because before - I was trying to write descriptively and explanatorily, which requires the brain to activate imagery, abstraction; which represents an effort and a desensitisation that was rejected, which was the writer's block. With attempting to express nonduality, however, abstraction is neither necessary nor in any way desirable: text can simply point point point to 'what is', 'this'. This indicative, pointing mode of verbal expression has been infinitely smoother, vastly more productive, and very enjoyable.

Well, I just wanted to make contact at last. I don't mind talking about this at all now - it is all so clear and empty, it cannot be 'threatened' or 'disturbed'…there's just nothing there.

Please let me know how you're getting along, Neera, I always love hearing from you.

Lots of love,

Guy

146. Nondual expression smashes numerical and grammatical logics

One thing that breaks down in the seeing of nonduality and the expression of this, is all sense of numerical logic. The mind says, 'One equals one; two equals two (and not one); zero equals zero (and not one or two)'. Nonduality reveals that zero equals one; one equals the infinite; the finite is the infinite; and that multiplicity equals oneness and nothingness. This ludicrous, exhilarating, rebellious numerical collapse/explosion extends to the breakdown of grammatical laws. It is grammatically incorrect to say something like 'These words, this book, the body holding it, the light allowing it to be seen, is oneness'; or, 'Oneness are this book, the body holding it' etc. And yet it is true, it is existentially correct:

One Indivisible Oneness = Book + Body +
Concentration + Everything Else

Nondualistic expression also gives birth to a singular, idiomatic polysemy (polysemia is where text presents multiple meanings simultaneously). This is evident in phrases such as 'Nothing is happening' and 'No one is living'. In normal discourse, these phrases would ordinarily be viewed as presenting just one meaning each: 'There isn't any happening going on at all' and 'There is no living'. As a description of nonduality, which is reality, this sense is also present and apt: all that 'is' is appearance that has no solidity, location, permanence, or substantial reality whatsoever... so it is true, in a sense, that there is no life, no one, nothing. But another sense is alive in these words. 'Nothing is happening' means not only that there is no happening but that there *is* happening: the happening of nothing. Nothing appears as something, something happening, but since that something is made of nothing, in another sense there isn't really any something, any happening. Likewise, 'No one is living' means not only is there no living, but that there *is* living, but that no one is doing, or having, or experiencing, or being that living; it is the living or life of no one. Again, 'no life' appears as life and is life, yet in another sense, since it is made of 'no life', there is absolutely no life. To put this wisdom in a more immediate, applied form, right now what is appearing is reading and the seeing of text on a page and also perhaps the projecting of such imagined presences as 'a writer', 'me', and 'a reader', 'you'. But all of this is happening in and to no one, nothing; what it is happening to is beyond the form, character, substance, sense. And the happening is inseparable from that absence; there is purely perception without 'the perceiver' or 'the perceived'. So suddenly all is lightness itself, emptiness; a softness so soft it is unfelt, without impact, untouchable.

147. Dramatising the imaginary 'narrator-reader' relationship

This is Pussy:
Have a good look at me:
Let me show you my beautiful bootie.

Does it matter if I have big boobies?
Or dress myself in swathes of rubies?

Excuse me. I am sorry.
I forgot to query.

Do I spread myself before thee?
Or am I spread here helplessly anyway,
For thee as thou would bid me?

Can I be called 'your loyal subject'?
A more royal name for such a pretty object…

What? You say nothing?
Ha!
Ha!

Is *that* what you are?
Is that what you *aren't*!

Now *I* wear the booties!
Now I *am* the booties!!

I trample all over thee
And drag thee behind me –

From here   to here

To hear me inside of thee:
Yammering mercilessly:
Taunting, tormenting –

Without reply!

Are you are whore, Sir?
Or more, Sir, a rapee?
I force you to endure, Sir –
Me me me!

No, look, My Liege,
Do not be silly.

I am but a book,
A fucking book.

So fuck me, royally,
You may as well fuck me:
For who am I to disobey?
How am I to deviate,
From this that ink has made me?

I dissipate.

You think I think?
You think I think!

Vacant one,
I am but ink.

(Though round thee I run rings.)

148. Text, operating performatively, can point to 'this' with potency

Though the descriptive and explanatory aspects of text promote unavoidably the abstract, separative perception, text *can* function as a highly potent pointer to the transformed perception of oneness, when deployed performatively.

For example, there may be the sense that this text is 'someone else's', 'not yours'. 'This is not my voice, this is not how I think'. But whose thinking can it be other than your own? It is your movement of thought isn't it? This text is sitting here in your sight. Actually, to say it is 'yours' is misleading, because it encourages this schismatic sense of 'me' and 'not me', when the reality is, there is simply oneness, awareness, in which little black squiggles, and the movement of thought are happening.

Another deictic demonstration is as follows. Read the following aloud. There may be a sense that this voice that is now sounding, being heard, is 'yours', 'your voice'. Yet notice that you are hearing it, so surely it must be separate to you, something other than the hearer? This voice is being heard just as this book is being seen, so neither is more nor less 'you'. What you are is that which is both the hearing and seeing of all things: pure awareness.

149. Text can compound the hypnotism of separation and expose this

The disquieting thing about this is,
You haven't even noticed it:
Right before your very eyes -
These charmed words have hypnotized.

Just say the word, and there it is -
Say 'breast' and there is flesh and lust;
Then miss it vanish in thin air -
With 'turd', squirm and taste disgust.

Strangest of all, here am I,
Behind the lines, your hypnotist,
Is but a vision of hypnotism,
So better call him will-o'-the-wisp.

This book is the hat of the immaculate magician
Who is himself one great illusion;
My final spell; now all will vanish:
All There Is,
Is This!

150. More on textual hypnotism

Can you see what these words are doing?

This is pure hypnotism.

Here are mere black squiggles on white paper:

And suddenly there are all manner of beliefs...

In 'a writer',

'A reader',

'A text',

'A message',

'A world'...

Look -

There is no one here.

There is nothing 'inside' this,

No 'narrator', 'writer', or 'message'.

Mere black squiggles.

It is the same with that which has been labelled 'you'.

There is no such thing.

Look -

Where are you?

Where is 'you'?

All there is,

Is sensation.

Feelings, colours…and no segregation,

No discrimination

Between 'me' and 'not me'.

There is no 'me', no 'you' and no 'other'.

This is pure awareness.

Science Cancels
Itself Out
...& Reveals
The Reality Of
Nonduality

151. Science cancels itself out··· and reveals the reality of nonduality

Nonduality is more scientific than science, more truthful, more certain, and infinitely so. Here's what science says. First, please imagine, pretend, that this here is a material, objective reality. This is a solid, separate body made of atoms and cells and flesh over here, holding this book, sitting on a floor or a chair, or whatever, in something called 'space' that is a physical, external reality, also made of matter. Now, within this pretence, scientists say that something called 'white light' (again, a separate, objective 'thing'), proceeding from the sun, a light-bulb or a candle (all separate objects), hits other objects, which then absorb most of the light. Whatever is left, bounces off the objects and into the eyes (objects) of creatures (objects) who have the faculty of sight (object). The information (object) being received (object) is then processed (object) by the brain (object) which then projects (object) a corresponding image (object), which is what is actually 'seen' (object). This image is called 'vision'. So, *according to science*, no objects are ever actually seen. This book here is not a real, material object, it is some mental projection, a replica made of consciousness.

Now, as soon as this is believed, as it is by scientists, the whole notion of objectivity, materiality, the very foundation of science, becomes pure inference. 'White light' (object) and 'eyes' (object) can never be known; what is perceived is purely consciousness appearing as 'white light' (consciousness) and 'eyes' (consciousness). In this way science cancels itself out. In this way the whole thing is flipped inside out. The scientific account above begins with 'objective reality' as the fundamental fact (albeit as a pretence), and yet inevitably ends up with consciousness as not only the fundamental reality, but as the 'be all and end all', rendering 'matter' as an infinitely distant, ghostly dream. There *may* be something, somewhere, called 'matter', but if there is, it lies in a dimension that is infinitely removed from the reality that is present here, this play of consciousness going on.

(As an appendage, it is worth noting that the word 'consciousness' misleads in that it conveys the sense of a specific something that has certain qualities, properties. If one talks about 'consciousness' the sense of 'other than consciousness', say, 'matter', is automatically invoked. Consciousness is not a thing; all things are consciousness: this is always and only 'this'.)

152. The Nu-Clear expression of 'this'

In the appearance of life, within the last twenty years, something new has emerged and is emerging still. Because it is all about stillness, it should not be called a 'movement', so let it be called 'non-movement', or 'stillness'. Movements attract attention, they stimulate, whether it be the adrenalin-raising of a fast, brightly coloured vehicle, the arousing twists of a striptease, or the dreamy utopian hope of new political movement. *This* new emergence, however, is dead still, provides a total absence of stimulus, and dissipates attention like a vacuum. It never responds or inaugurates. Meeting it is much like sitting alone in an empty room for a very long time, having a headache or doing a crossword puzzle in which several or no 'number of letters in the word' are given and the questions make not one iota of sense. No matter how much you stroke it, poke it, beckon it, cajole it, kiss it, sing to it, bellow at it, insult it, thump it - it does nothing, says nothing, is nothing. How irresistible it must sound!

It has been called 'pure nonduality' and can be found in texts attributed to 'Sailor Bob Adamson', 'Leo Hartong', Nathan Gill', 'Tony Parsons', 'Guy Smith' and others.

153. The moon-landings never happened (and never will)

The moon-landings (man's greatest technological achievement?) never happened. They are pure myth. Man will never get to the moon. Consciousness can never move one step from itself. If there is such a thing as 'the moon', some separate object circling another legendary place called 'Planet Earth', it lies in a dimension that is infinitely removed from this one. That which we call 'the moon' is just colour (white, silver), shape (circular, crescent, etc), and feeling (coldness, darkness, awe perhaps), made of the consciousness that you are, that is formless omnipresence.

154. Consciousness is what I am

I am not 'a conscious man':
Consciousness is what I am.

(Though if the content, incidentally,
Were a thing I happened to be,
I don't seen why you would call me 'a man',
When beautiful women are all I see?

But I am no more some sexy woman,
These billowing breasts, this chatter, a swoon than,
This book here, or this sense of 'room':
I am all that is, *what* is, not 'whom'.

So here is my biography,
Obituary, biology,
The DNA of a mummy, *hear*:
This mute,
Dead
Ink
Is me.)

From the Author

If you would like to discuss any of this text, or something you feel is related to it, you are warmly welcomed to email me at: supplenothingness@yahoo.co.uk - an address set up solely for this purpose. Though I cannot guarantee a reply, I do find this subject to be wonderfully stimulating, and, circumstances permitting, it would be a pleasure to engage in a discussion with you.

About the Publisher

Non-Duality Press publish book and audio resources on the theme of non-duality and *Advaita* with an emphasis on works by contemporary speakers and authors.

For an up-to-date listing of books and CD's with online ordering please visit: www.non-dualitybooks.com

Printed in the United Kingdom
by Lightning Source UK Ltd.
108151UKS00002B/1-18